Kindom  Encounters

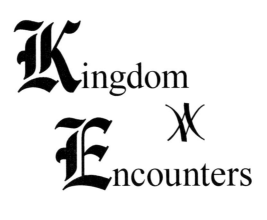

Kingdom Encounters

RICHARD A. SODMONT

iUniverse, Inc.
Bloomington

Kingdom Encounters

All scripture quotations are from the New International Version of the Bible, copyright 1990 by Zondervan.

iUniverse books may be ordered through booksellers or by contacting:

iUniverse
1663 Liberty Drive
Bloomington, IN 47403
www.iuniverse.com
1-800-Authors (1-800-288-4677)

ISBN: 978-1-4759-6865-1 (sc)
ISBN: 978-1-4759-6867-5 (hc)
ISBN: 978-1-4759-6866-8 (e)

Library of Congress Control Number: 2012923956

Printed in the United States of America

iUniverse rev. date: 12/26/2012

Contents

Foreword

Rick Sodmont is a passionate lover of God who desires to challenge all believers to know and encounter the living Christ. Rick has obediently answered the call on his life and walks in character, integrity, love, and the wisdom of God. He shares many testimonies and experiences from his life and ministry to encourage others to seek God for their own kingdom experiences. Rick's journey of intimacy has allowed him to build and strengthen his relationship with God and increase his level of faith, hope, and love. It is through this intimacy we learn to know him. As we learn to know him we learn to trust, which allows us to receive all he has for us.

Kingdom Encounters provides a roadmap to help fulfill destiny in our lives. It changes how we see the King and his kingdom. It reveals how powerful our testimonies are in changing the atmosphere of our circumstances. Rick's quest invited Holy visitations, which increased his faith, revelation of who God is and his kingdom principles. Rick presents God's desire for an intimate relationship with each of us. Each testimony provides an opportunity for us to experience God in new ways. Anticipate an encounter into the realms of his glory. Only believe … you can experience God's fullness in your life! May you be blessed as you read this book and encounter the King and his kingdom.

Bill Chilcote
My Father's House Ministries International Inc.

Kingdom Encounters is an eye-opening, heart-touching collection of Rick's supernatural experiences with God. His life stories will also challenge you to believe that what God has done in his word, he is still doing. It is amazing that Christians believe that the children of Israel walked through the Red Sea, Elijah was caught up in a whirlwind into the heavens, Jesus walked on water and healed the sick … yet those same Christians struggle to believe that miracles like those could still happen today. This book will increase your faith and inspire you to reach for another realm of his glory.

My wife, LuAnne, traveled with Randy Clark and the Global Awakening team along with Rick to Brazil and Africa. She was there in the meetings sitting beside him during his God encounters, where he was caught up into the heavens. God used him in a powerful way on the team because of these God experiences. Rick helped her gain a greater understanding of the supernatural and spiritual warfare.

It was very difficult even for Apostles Paul and John to describe heavenly encounters with earthly words; yet we gain glimpses of God's glory and a revelation of Jesus Christ. As you read through this book, realize that Rick is describing his heavenly experiences to the best of his ability. I encourage every reader to be slow to judge and quick to gain from Rick's experiences, remembering that the book of Revelation is very unique as well. Let God take you higher.

Dale and LuAnne Mast—pastors of Destiny Christian Church in Dover, DE, Eagle Fire Ministries, and Eagle Fire Network. LuAnne Mast is author of *God, I Feel Like Cinderella*!

Introduction

What is reality? Is reality limited to what we have been taught by our parents, our schools, or perhaps even our churches? Can reality be defined only by that which we can touch, see, smell, or experience with our physical senses? Are there other realities that exist, perhaps even supernatural ones, beyond our physical limitations?

Is it possible that angels and demons really do exist? If so, what is their purpose? Could there really be a Creator out there? Does he care about us as individuals? Is he actively involved in the affairs of the earth? What possibilities exist beyond our present paradigms? Are we willing to explore these other possibilities? Are you ready to recognize that this book is written for you?

As I share numerous testimonies throughout this book, I pray that you, the reader, would be open to changing the way you think about these things. And though I share these testimonies as mine, I want you to realize that this book is not about me.

This book is about the awesome God that I love and serve. It's about his great love for all mankind and his desire to radically change people's lives. The testimonies you are about to read are his testimonies. They reveal his love, grace, power, and goodness. They reveal his true nature and character. They reveal the only true king and his kingdom.

I also want to state that I have done my best to accurately represent these encounters and the words that the Lord spoke to me. After experiencing each of these encounters, I immediately recorded them in writing so that I would have an accurate account of these events. I have also asked the Holy Spirit to remind me of those things and to fill in any gaps in my memory. So let's get started.

Throughout the history of mankind, God has been intimately involved in the lives of people. Many people have had supernatural experiences and encounters with God. Many such experiences are recorded in the pages of the Bible. And many people have shared their encounters over the years through books and other media.

In a previous book, *The Father's Love,* I shared an encounter that happened to me in 2002 while I was on a mission trip to Belem, Brazil. During that encounter God opened my eyes to see into the spiritual realm. I saw God descend from heaven on his throne, and he spoke directly to me and revealed his great love for me. It was one of many powerful experiences that I have had with God, and it was one that radically changed my life.

Contained within the pages of this book are some of the other life-changing encounters that I have experienced since that time. As you read them, you will be challenged in your faith to believe God for things that you previously dismissed as false or as fiction. You will be challenged to shift your own paradigm. I encourage you to approach this book with an open heart and mind to receive all that God has for you.

I will share encounters with you that I have had directly with God, and some that I have had with angels and others with demons. I will share with you some of the out-of-body experiences that I have had. I will share things that I have seen in the spiritual realm. I will share things that God has spoken directly to me. And I will also share some of the revelation that I have received as a result of these encounters.

Allow me to share some scriptures with you to give you a precedent for these things. Many people have never experienced these things and have never been taught about them, so they have a hard time believing them. But what does the Bible say about them?

In 2 Kings 6, the king of Aram had sent horses, chariots, and a large force of men to surround the Israelites in the city of Dothan. Early in the morning, Elisha's servant went outside and saw this huge army that was surrounding them. He became fearful and asked Elisha what they were going to do. Notice Elisha's reply.

> 2 Kings 6:16–17: "Don't be afraid," the prophet answered. "Those who are with us are more than those who are with them." And Elisha prayed, "O Lord, open his eyes so he may see." Then the Lord opened the servant's eyes, and he looked and saw the hills full of horses and chariots of fire all around Elisha.

Elisha had been given a "seer" anointing. He had been given the ability to see into the spiritual realm. Then he prayed for God to open his servant's eyes also, and God did. There are many people in the scriptures who had the ability to see into that realm. And there are still people today who have that ability.

As a matter of fact, the spiritual realm is a greater reality than the physical realm. Not only is it a greater reality, but it is also a superior reality. Let me give you an example of what I mean by this. It is a reality that sickness and disease exist upon the earth. But the greater, far superior reality is that we can be healed of those things because of what Jesus accomplished on the cross.

Going back to the scripture in 2 Kings 6, you will see that the armies of the Lord, the spiritual realm, blinded the armies of the king of Aram, the physical realm.

According to 2 Corinthians 4:4, what is seen is temporary, but what is unseen is eternal. Forces are at work all around us every day that most people do not see or even acknowledge, but they are still there.

Ephesians 6:12: For our struggle is not against flesh and blood, but against the rulers, against the authorities, against the powers of this dark world and against the spiritual forces of evil in the heavenly realms.

Hebrews 1:14: Are not all angels ministering spirits sent to serve those who will inherit salvation?

Angels and demons are real. The spiritual realm is real and actually coexists with the physical realm. Angels and demons work within that realm to affect our lives every day. Angels minister for our good while demons are trying to destroy us. Though most people do not see them, they are there. I believe every believer has been given the ability to see into and/or enter into the spiritual realm. Consider the experience of the Apostle Paul.

2 Corinthians 12:1–4: I must go on boasting. Although there is nothing to be gained, I will go on to visions and revelations from the Lord. I know a man in Christ who fourteen years ago was caught up to the third heaven. Whether it was in the body or out of the body I do not know—God knows. And I know that

> this man—whether in the body or apart from the body I do not know, but God knows—was caught up to paradise. He heard inexpressible things, things that a man is not permitted to tell.

I believe Paul was speaking about himself here in this scripture. He was talking about actually being taken up into heaven, to paradise. He wasn't sure if he was in his body or out of it, but he was sure that he was taken there. And while he was there, God gave him many wonderful revelations. I believe this is where Paul received the revelation of God's grace that he speaks about throughout the New Testament.

> Galatians 1:11–12: I want you to know, brothers, that the gospel I preached is not something that man made up. I did not receive it from any man, nor was I taught it; I received it by revelation from Jesus Christ.

Paul was not the only one who was caught up to the heavens. The Apostle John was also taken up and saw many awesome things. The entire book of Revelation is John's account of what he saw and heard.

> Revelation 1:9–10: I, John, your brother and companion in the suffering and kingdom and patient endurance that are ours in Jesus, was on the island of Patmos because of the word of God and the testimony of Jesus. On the Lord's

day I was in the Spirit, and I heard behind me a loud voice like a trumpet.

Revelation 4:1–2: After this I looked, and there before me was a door standing open in heaven. And the voice I had first heard speaking to me like a trumpet said, "Come up here, and I will show you what must take place after this." At once I was in the Spirit, and there before me was a throne in heaven with someone sitting on it.

If Paul and John were allowed to enter into the spiritual realm, what makes us think that we can't? God loves us all the same and scripture says that he does not show favoritism. I believe that everything I find in the scriptures is available to me. And because of my belief, I have encounters with God in the spiritual realm on a regular basis.

I want to encourage you to seek God for personal encounters in your life. He desires to have an intimate relationship with all of us. And when you have a relationship with someone, you experience their presence. If you don't, then you don't really have much of a relationship.

God is tired of religion and religious practices. He wants people to know him personally and to experience his presence, power, and glory in their lives. From Genesis to Revelation, the Bible is filled with people who had personal encounters with God. He desires the same for us. He is a God that does not change.

I am asking you to lay down some of your former religious beliefs and seek the Lord with all of your heart. When you truly experience his presence and power, you will never be the same. You will never again be content with "life as usual." You will desire more and more of him. You will become more and more like him.

I pray that all who read this book will truly have "encounters" with the living God and never be the same! I pray that you will receive revelation, that you might know Jesus better. I pray that the eyes of your heart will be enlightened, that you will know the hope to which he has called you. And I pray that God will increase your faith, that you would believe him for the impossible.

Most of all, I pray that you would realize how much your Father in heaven loves you and desires to be ever so close to you.

Chapter 1
The House of Intimacy

One day back in 2002, I was lying on my living room floor seeking the Lord. I had some soft worship music playing in the background. I so enjoy these times of intimacy with the Lord, and I always expect to encounter him in some way. I was asking God to reveal himself to me that I might know him better. I was asking for more of his power and glory to be revealed in my life.

I heard the Lord call to me to "come up here," and I suddenly found myself racing up through the clouds into the heavenly realms. It felt as if I was shot out of a cannon. I could feel the wind rushing by at incredible speeds. Like Paul, I do not know if I was in the body or out of it. I ended up standing in front of a very large house. Jesus was standing at the front door beckoning me to enter the house with him. This is the record of what I saw and experienced.

As we entered the house, I could feel the glory of God all around me. It was so powerful that I could hardly stand. The air was so thick that it seemed as if you could feel the weight of it on your shoulders. A white brilliance in the room nearly blinded me.

Directly in front of me was a long corridor with doors on both sides. The walls were a brilliant white color but otherwise plain, without pictures or any other decoration. At the far end of the corridor I noticed a set of stairs that led upward.

Jesus walked over to the first door and walked right through it without opening it. He then called to me to come in with him. I walked over to the door, but there wasn't a doorknob on it to open it. I wondered how I was going to get in. Then Jesus said, "By faith." I thought, "Well, okay," and then walked right through the door just as Jesus had. It was as if I could feel the composition of the door itself passing right through my body.

We were standing in a very large room lined with rows of shelving that were full of human body parts. Though the room was confined by walls, it seemed to have no walls, which gave me the feeling that it could grow as needed, without limitations. The shelves were almost transparent like glass, but distinguishable one from the other.

Eyes, ears, hearts, arms, legs, kidneys—all parts of the human body—were stacked on these shelves in various colors, shapes, and sizes, representing every size of person from infant to adult, and every race of people on the face of the earth.

Though I am at a loss for words to accurately describe what they looked like, it was as if each part had been freshly created, yet without the life of the blood in it until it could be distributed to the specific individual that it was intended for on the earth.

I could hardly believe what I was seeing. Though I know that I didn't yet fully understand what I was experiencing, I felt as though the possibility of bringing healing to people I knew and even those I had yet to meet had just drastically increased. I was overwhelmed with excitement!

Then Jesus spoke to me and said that if I would remain humble and have faith in him, that I could enter this room anytime I wanted and get whatever part someone needed for their healing.

Can you imagine how much God loves you, that he has already made provision for the healing of your physical body? Can we as individuals grasp how fully God has equipped us to be able to bring healing to others?

We then continued on to another room. It was full of the gifts of the Spirit. They were embodied in words and carried the essence of each particular gift, floating around the room in the air like helium balloons. There was prophecy, tongues, wisdom, words of knowledge, interpretation of tongues, discerning of spirits, faith, working of miracles, healing, administration, serving, generosity, teaching, and love—lots of love. I could feel the love of God engulfing me.

Again the Lord said to me that if I would remain humble and have faith, I could enter this room anytime I wanted to get whatever gift was needed at that moment for ministry.

I had always believed that God determined what gifts people received (1 Corinthians 12:11). But I now believe, based on this experience, that by faith we have access to all of the spiritual gifts, because the giver of the gifts lives inside of us. Though God has determined our predominate gifts, we are not limited to only those gifts. Hallelujah!

We then left that room and went into the next. It was filled with the fruit of the Spirit. There was love, joy, peace, patience, kindness, goodness, faithfulness, gentleness, and self-control. With every breath I took in that room, I was breathing in this fruit and exhaling flesh. Inhaling was like holding a pie under your nose and almost being able to taste it by its aroma. When exhaling, it felt like everything in me that was not in line with these gifts was being expelled from my body, like a deep sigh of relief.

I could tell I was being transformed from the inside out. Jesus said to me that the more time I spend intimately with him, the more these fruit would become a part of my being and enable me to help others.

We exited that room and started down the corridor again. To my surprise, we bypassed a room and went on to the next one. I asked Jesus why we had skipped that room. He said it was because I wasn't ready to deal with that room. The enemy still occupies that room. Then I realized that the house we were touring was the temple of the Lord, my own human body.

I came to realize that though much of me was being occupied by God, areas of my life were still under the influence of the enemy. Jesus had said that the kingdom of God was within us (Luke 17:21). I now have a new understanding of that scripture. Whenever we surrender any area of our lives to the Lord, the enemy loses his influence over that area, and the Lord then fills it with a piece of heaven, a piece of God's kingdom.

Whenever we first come to Christ, the enemy has control over, or at least influences, many, if not all, of the areas of our lives. He influences our flesh, our thinking, and our beliefs. Because he controls our thinking, he also controls our actions. Our actions will always follow our beliefs. But as we grow in Christ and become mature, the enemy loses more and more of his control over us, which allows God to fill us with more and more of his kingdom.

We are delivered from the power of the enemy, and we begin to walk more and more in the Spirit. As we continue to walk in the truth and power of the Spirit, we reap the good fruit of the kingdom of heaven. But if we revert to walking in the flesh, then the door is opened for the enemy to come back into our lives and begin to control us again.

When Moses led the Israelites out of Egypt, God told him that he was going to lead them into the Promised Land, the land of Canaan. It was a land flowing with milk and honey. The problem was that the enemy occupied all of the land God promised to Israel. God told them that he would drive all the inhabitants out of the land, as long as Israel walked in obedience to him.

If you follow the history of the Israelites, you see that when they were obedient, God gave them great victory over the enemy, and Israel occupied the new territory. But when they disobeyed, they were defeated, and the enemy remained in control of the land. A perfect example of this is their defeat at Ai because of Achan's sin. See Joshua 7.

So it is in our lives. The more we surrender the control of our lives over to God and walk in obedience to him, the more of his kingdom that is imparted to us, and the more we experience the fruit of his kingdom. But the enemy remains in control of any area of our lives that we do not give to God, and we live defeated in them.

It is important to remember that the Holy Spirit determines when it is time to deal with these areas of our lives. If we try to deal with them apart from him, we will usually fail.

Jesus then led me through another door. It was full of what I consider to be the very nature and character of God. There was love, grace, mercy, and compassion. But there was also judgment, righteousness, and justice. There was goodness and faithfulness, but also wrath. I couldn't actually "see" anything in this room; he was the room! I was in the very presence of God, and every characteristic that makes him who he is encompassed me like a blanket.

I knew that my presence in this room would bring me closer to becoming more like Jesus because when we are in his presence we are changed. It was like he became a part of me, and I became a part of him. I began to understand his ways better than ever before. I knew that he was molding me more and more into his image. This was totally awesome! I also knew that intimacy was the key to developing the very life of God within me.

The last room that we entered on that floor was full of weapons. Although I did not anticipate what was in this room, I also wasn't surprised by it, because it is part of the provision that God has made for us. I felt terribly excited because I knew that I could use these weapons to slay the enemy, much like a hunter uses a gun to slay a bear.

There was the sword of the Spirit, which is the Word of God, both logos and rhema. There was truth, which sets men free. There was worship and intercession. There was the blood of the Lamb and the words of our testimony. There was the cross, and resurrection power. There was the helmet of salvation, the breastplate of righteousness, and the gospel of peace. There was the shield of faith.

All of these were the main headings listed on the ends of rows of shelving. And suspended in midair over all the shelves was the word love, depicting how God's love enables us to utilize these spiritual weapons. I saw shelves full of various types of weapons: swords, spears, bows and arrows, bombs, guns, lasers, hand grenades, and missiles. The shelving row that had faith listed on it was full of shields, body armor, and protective clothing. I knew that no weapon formed against me would prosper as long as I had faith.

This room is not for the faint of heart. It is for the true warrior brides who are willing to lay down their lives for the sake of the King. It is for the passionate lovers of Christ, because only true love will motivate us to lay down our lives for someone else. This room is for the living army of the living Christ.

It is not for those who are deceived into thinking that there is no war. It is not for those who choose to remain prisoners of war. It is for those who choose to escape the prison camps of the enemy and who will then turn around and fight to set others free. It is for those who will inflict great damage on the enemy's kingdom. It is for those who are willing to take the kingdom by force.

As sons and daughters of God, we have been given authority on this earth to use all of these weapons to build the kingdom of God and to destroy the work of the devil. If the church of Jesus Christ ever discovers the firepower that is available to us, then the kingdom of darkness will be in great trouble. Jesus told me to tell others about these rooms, in hopes that they too would enter by faith and be equipped to live a godly life and fight the good fight of faith.

We then proceeded up the stairway, which was tremendously inviting. With each step we climbed, the glory of the Lord increased. The weightiness of his glory caused my legs to weaken, making it more and more difficult to take the next step. It was like climbing a mountain with lead weights tied to each leg. When we reached the top, we turned into the outer chamber of the bedroom. I suddenly realized that this is what Jesus desired the most, to have a close relationship with me, like that which exists between a husband and wife.

He desired to show me his love and affection in a way that would touch my heart and soul and awaken my spirit to become one with him.

It is through this intimacy with him that we receive all things. He reveals himself to us and shows us his will for our lives. He empowers us to be his witnesses and to fulfill our callings. He sets us free from the bondages to the enemy. He gives us revelation about himself and the scriptures. But it all starts with intimacy through relationship.

When I stepped into the outer chamber, I immediately fell facedown on the floor. My awareness of his glory was so powerful that I thought I was going to die. It was both beautiful and terrifying. My spirit was aching to be with Jesus, but my flesh was screaming at me to get out of there.

I looked up at Jesus, and he was beckoning me to come into the bedroom with him. I tried several times to crawl across the floor into the bedroom, but I was overcome by feelings of unworthiness.

I thought to myself, "I don't deserve to be intimate with the King of Glory. How could a wretch like me ever even think about being in the same room with him, let alone being intimate with him?" Knowing my thoughts, Jesus said to me, "If you are not worthy to be here, then I died for nothing." The truth of his statement cut me to the very core of my being. Again he beckoned me to enter with him.

But the brilliance of his glory was overwhelming to me, and my flesh would not allow me to get any closer on this occasion. Though my spirit was willing, my flesh was weak. I crawled back out of the room in shame. I could see the disappointment on the face of Jesus. He so desired to be intimate with me. He wanted to reveal himself and the Father to me in ways I had never known before. I was in tears, and so was he, as I left the room. I asked him to forgive me and hoped that I would have another opportunity to be with him in this way.

Immediately, I found myself back on my living room floor. I was both greatly excited over what I had just experienced and deeply saddened that I missed out on what Jesus wanted the most.

Since that time, I have received further revelation that has helped to release me so that now I am not ashamed to enter into his presence. I no longer feel unworthy, and I no longer have a guilty conscience that hinders me from entering God's presence. One of the key verses that helped me overcome this fear is found in the book of Hebrews.

> Hebrews 10:19–22: Therefore, brothers, since we have confidence to enter the Most Holy Place by the blood of Jesus, by a new and living way opened for us through the curtain, that is, his body, and since we have a great high priest over the house of God, let us draw near to God with a sincere heart in full assurance of faith, having our hearts sprinkled to cleanse us from a guilty conscience and having our bodies washed with pure water.

The only thing that gives us confidence, cleanses our guilty conscience, and makes us worthy to enter into the very presence of God is the blood of Jesus!

I pray that you would realize that you also are made worthy by his blood and you also may enter his presence and commune with him anytime you choose.

Chapter 2
Encounter in Joao Pessoa, Brazil

In his book *Open My Eyes, Lord*, Gary Oates mentions an encounter that I had with the Lord during a mission trip to Brazil in December 2002. Here are the complete details of that encounter.

During the evening service, Gary Oates was speaking, and he asked for members of the ministry team to come forward to give words of knowledge. When he did, I felt the Spirit of God come upon me very powerfully, and I began to shake all through my body. I was trembling as I walked up onto the stage and over to the microphone to give the word. But an overwhelming wave of God's presence came into the room, and I fell to the floor under the power of God.

The Lord spoke to me and said, "Come up here." I replied, "I can't God." I didn't know how to make myself go to heaven. Just then God sent two angels to escort me. They took on bodily form and were dressed in white robes. They picked me up, and suddenly we went soaring up through the clouds. Like before, we traveled at great speed, and I could feel and hear the wind rushing past my body.

As we ascended, I looked down and saw my body still trembling on the stage. My soul and spirit were heading for heaven while my physical body remained on the earth.

When we came to a stop, I found myself standing directly in front of God the Father as he was seated on his throne. I was both terrified and excited at the same time. What an awesome sight he was to behold! He looked both ancient and young at the same time. His hair was white as snow but his "flesh" was like that of a newborn baby. Light was emanating from within him, like looking directly into the sun.

The Bible declares that we are made up of body, soul, and spirit (1 Thessalonians 5:23). Our body is simply that, our physical body composed of bone and flesh. Our soul is made up of our mind, will, and emotions. Our spirit is the life force within us. It is the part of us that becomes one with the Spirit of God when we are born again.

My body was left on the earth, and now my soul and spirit were standing in front of the Creator of the universe. My soul and spirit then began to separate. My spirit looked like a "clean," transparent glass figure of me, while my soul was like a "dirty," opaque image of me. My spirit was standing a couple of feet behind my soul, which was about ten feet away from God.

Just prior to going on this trip, the Lord had revealed to me that I had been incorrectly judging him and also that I had become very judgmental of other Christians. I had asked him to forgive me and had also apologized to some of the people that I had judged. I knew that God had forgiven me, but I still felt dirty. I was shocked that I had been committing this sin for so long and hadn't even realized it.

Now, as I was standing in front of him, I felt so unclean. As my spirit man looked at my soul, I saw two large chains wrapped around my soul, which were holding a large trunk full of garbage to my back. God then took his sword and swung it right across my shoulders and through my neck. I thought my head was going to fall off.

To my surprise, his sword had cut through the chains but hadn't harmed my neck in any way. The trunk full of garbage fell off my back, as did the chains. I felt a tremendous relief from the weight that I had carried for so long. That bondage was suddenly and entirely gone, and I felt so much relief and freedom!

However, as I looked at my soul from behind, I could still see a lot of dirt and garbage stuck to my back. The Father then told the two angels to wash me under the waterfall. I watched them carry my soul over to the waterfall and hold me under it. The river of heaven just poured down over me. The cool water was so refreshing and so cleansing. I have never felt so clean. The angels then carried my "clean" soul (which now looked just like my spirit) back over to the Father, where it was reunited with my spirit.

Then the Father said he wanted to show me something. He opened up his chest, and I could see his heart. I could feel the great love that he has for all mankind. I began to understand just how much he loves people. It is impossible for me to describe that love to you because it far surpasses all human understanding! But it was the most amazing love that I have ever experienced. I wept over his great love.

Then God said that his greatest desire was to be with us and to have us with him. He said he loves mankind just as much as he loves Jesus (John 17:23). He said that it is his desire to come back and take us all home to be with him, but he is holding back so that everyone will have the opportunity to be saved.

Then he gave me a message for his people. He told me to preach this message everywhere I go:

> Tell my people to wake up. Tell them to wake up. There are many in the church who are sleeping. They honor me with their lips, but their hearts are far from me. They go through the motions, but few have entered into intimacy with me. They have a form of religion, but few actually live in relationship with me. Tell

them that what I desire the most is to have an intimate relationship with each one of them.

I don't want their religious activities. I want a relationship. I want the kind of relationship that exists between a husband and wife. I am your husband, and you are my bride. Tell them that I love them all very much, and I have no greater desire than to be intimate with each one of them.

And then, out of that intimacy, I will empower them to be my witnesses and send them out to reach those who need Jesus Christ. The quicker you enter this relationship, the quicker you will be empowered and sent forth. The quicker you go forth, the quicker the world will be won. And then I will come and take you home. I would love to come and take you back with me now, but the moment I do, I will be condemning millions of people to eternal damnation in hell.

For those who choose to enter into that intimacy now, I will come and fellowship with them and be intimate with them even now. So tell my children to wake up. This is the message I have for my people, to enter into intimacy with me.

Suddenly, I found myself back in my body, still lying on the stage trembling. The entire encounter had lasted almost an hour.

That was a pretty sobering message. I know that many people feel they are living in a relationship with God. They fulfill all the requirements of their particular religion or denomination, but do they really know God? Are they truly living in an intimate relationship with him? I can't answer that question for anyone but myself. I can only encourage all of you to really consider where you are in your relationship with God.

God desires so much more than mere religion or religious activities. He desires to reveal himself to us that we might know him personally and intimately. He desires to set us free from the things that so easily entangle us. He desires to empower us and send us out to win the world over to him.

It's time for us to wake up and be whom he called us to be and fulfill what he called us to do. Let's not be like the Pharisees and teachers of the law of Jesus's day, who were very religious but didn't even recognize Christ when he came to them.

Mark 7:6–9:

He replied, "Isaiah was right when he prophesied about you hypocrites; as it is written:

'These people honor me with their lips, but
their hearts are far from me. They worship me
in vain; their teachings are but rules taught by
men.'

"You have let go of the commands of God and
are holding on to the traditions of men."

And he said to them, "You have a fine way of
setting aside the commands of God in order
to observe your own traditions."

Jesus went on to say that they nullified the word of God
by their own traditions, which they have handed down.
And I believe many people in the church today follow the
traditions of their church but really don't know God. It time
for us to truly enter into intimacy with him. That's what he
desires the most.

I pray that now is the time for all of you to stop going
through the motions of religion and start entering into a real,
intimate relationship with Jesus. I pray that you encounter
the reality of Jesus, not just the facts about Jesus.

Chapter 3
Slaying the Serpent

In November 2003 I found myself on a mission trip to Ghana with Global Awakening. The trip was being led by Gary and Kathi Oates, who were associates with Global Awakening. There were twenty other people on the ministry team from the United States. We were ministering at a couple of churches around the cities of Accra and Tema.

This was some of the hardest ministry ground I have ever encountered. After three days of ministry, we had seen only one salvation, a few minor miracles, and a few deliverances. People appeared to be unresponsive to the gospel, or perhaps unresponsive to the American team. There seemed to be a major stronghold over that area that needed to be broken before we would see the glory of the Lord poured out.

One night just prior to our leaving for the evening service, I was discussing these things with a few of the team members in the hotel lobby. All of a sudden, the power of God came upon me, and I entered into this open vision. I slumped to the floor and remained there until the vision ended.

I was taken up into the spiritual realm, where I could look down on the entire nation of Ghana. It was as if I was on another planet looking through a telescope at Ghana. I saw a large green serpent with sharp fangs coiled up around the nation. It kept squeezing tighter and tighter, and I knew that it was squeezing the life out of that nation, especially the spiritual life of the church.

Also, a great battle was going on in the spiritual realm between the angels of God and the demons. Angels with swords and other weapons were fighting against demons in the atmosphere over Ghana. You could hear their swords clashing and see "spiritual blood" pouring out of those who had been slain, representing the defeat of that spirit, angelic or demonic. God had even sent Michael the archangel to make war against this serpent.

As soon as Michael engaged the serpent, the serpent coiled up around Michael's wrist, causing him to drop his sword. Then it coiled up around the rest of his body and began squeezing the life out of him. I was in shock. If Michael could not defeat this serpent, what chance did mere men like us have?

I asked God what was going on. He told me that the outcome of this battle would be determined by his people in Ghana. I asked him what he meant by that. He said that if his people would humble themselves, repent of their ways, and turn back to him, he would empower Michael and the other angels to win this battle. I still did not fully understand what he meant.

He told me that he loved the people of Ghana and that he wanted to pour out his glory over that nation. He said that like the Israelites, the people of Ghana had lived in bondage for hundreds of years, but now he was coming to lead them out of captivity and into the promised land. He also said that the choice would be theirs. If they choose to forgive, then his glory would be poured out.

I asked God who they needed to forgive and why. He said that the serpent I saw over Ghana was a spirit of hatred toward Americans. I asked him why the people of Ghana hated us so much. He said because Ghana was one of the nations that Americans would go to and get slaves to bring back to America. Many families and lives had been ripped apart, and many people in Ghana still harbored bitterness and unforgivingness toward Americans.

I asked God what we needed to do to break the stronghold of hatred over this nation. He said that he wanted the entire American team to repent in front of the entire congregation for all of the atrocities that Americans had committed against the people of Ghana. He said that if the people of

Ghana would choose to forgive us, then the power of that serpent would be broken, and the heavens would be opened over Ghana.

I shared the vision with Gary and Kathi, the leaders of the team. I had previously learned the importance of submitting to authority—that we only have authority in the heavenly realms as we are in submission to proper authority here on earth. The decision of what to do with this vision would be theirs. Thankfully, they decided that we needed to do what God had shown in the vision.

At the next service, the entire American team, led by Gary, got on our knees in front of the whole congregation and repented for all of the atrocities that our forefathers had committed against the people of Ghana. The Spirit of God came over all of us, and we were in tears as we confessed ours sins before God and man. Although Gary led us, each of us spoke aloud to the people of Ghana and repented for taking slaves, rape, murder, abuse, and many other sins. It was a powerful experience.

A few of the pastors and church leaders came forward and declared that they had forgiven us. Many in the congregation also forgave us. Many tears were flowing in both groups of people. People came forward and began hugging us and speaking forgiveness to us.

As soon as they spoke forgiveness to us, I felt a major breakthrough in the spiritual realm, like the shifting of two tectonic plates in the earth. God opened my spiritual eyes again, and I saw Michael taking his sword and cutting off the head of the serpent. The stronghold of hatred had been destroyed.

During the next three days of ministry, 353 people gave their lives to Jesus, as compared to only one during the first three days. Thirty-five blind or visually impaired people received their sight back. Twenty-two deaf or hearing-impaired people received their hearing back. Numerous other people were healed of various sicknesses and diseases. Many others were delivered from the power of the enemy.

At the end of the trip, we were discussing why we felt the trip had changed for the better. Some felt it was simply because we had moved to a different venue. But my belief is that it was because the stronghold over that nation was taken down as we sought the Lord in prayer and obeyed what he had shown us to do.

I have put this principle into practice various times since then, and I have seen God tear down other strongholds so that his kingdom could be established here on the earth, as it is in heaven. I will be sharing other examples of seeking the Lord in intercession and walking in obedience to him throughout this book.

My prayer is that as you encounter strongholds of the enemy in your own lives you would ask the Lord to show you how to overcome them, believe in what he says, and obey him, that you also might see breakthrough.

Chapter 4
The Book of Life

This encounter happened on the same ministry trip to Ghana in 2003 that I mentioned in the previous chapter. As I was sleeping one night, I saw Jesus riding on a white horse in the heavenly realms. He was dressed in a white robe with a purple sash around him.

People often ask me what Jesus looks like. I can best describe him like this: I believe he appears to people in a way that person would recognize him as Jesus. Whatever the mental picture of Jesus is in you, he appears to you that way so you can recognize that it's him. For me, Jesus appears as he looked on a picture that I saw many times while growing up.

He beckoned to me to come to him. I noticed that he had a second white horse with him without a rider. I assumed it was for me. The next thing I knew, I was sitting on the other white horse next to Jesus. Whether I was in the body or out of the body, I do not know.

Jesus then asked me how it was going. I couldn't even answer him. I was too afraid to speak. But I thought to myself that this mission trip has been pretty difficult on me. It was probably the most difficult one I've been on so far. I spent most of the trip limping around in severe pain with gout in my feet. Jesus repeated my thoughts to me, which totally amazed me. He continued to talk to me as though we were best friends. It was quite some time before I was able to speak in reply to him, but it didn't matter since he could read my thoughts.

We rode along conversing for a while, until we reached the gates of heaven. I couldn't begin to describe what I saw there because my full attention was on Jesus. We then rode inside the city and stopped at a building that looked somewhat like a castle. He took me inside the building and into a room that seemed to have no walls. In every direction that I looked, the only thing I could see was white.

In the middle of the room was a very large book. It was about ten feet wide and six feet high. It was opened up and sitting on a table. Jesus called me over and told me to look into the book. It looked like an atlas. On the left-hand page were North and South America. On the right-hand page were Europe, Asia, Africa, Australia, and the rest of the world.

Then Jesus told me to focus on the nation of Ghana, where I was presently ministering. As I did, I realized that the book was actually coming alive. As I focused in more and more, I began to see trees, buildings, animals, and people. It was like zooming in to the earth from a large telescope in outer space. I zoomed all the way in until I could see myself sleeping in a hotel in Ghana. This was incredible!

My curiosity and imagination began to run wild. I then decided to focus on America. I zoomed all the way in until I could see inside of my house in Hastings, Pennsylvania. I saw my wife, Tina, bathing my two youngest children, Jessica and Jacob. I saw my two oldest daughters, Stephanie and Robin, sitting at the kitchen table doing their homework. I was amazed. I took notice that it was about 2:00 a.m. in Ghana, which would have been around 9:00 p.m. in Hastings. I looked at Jesus and said, "Wow!"

He then began to explain to me that this book was the account of mankind from the first day of creation until the end of the earth. He said that each page in the book contains one day in the history of the world. All of the history of the world is recorded in this book.

Jesus also began to explain to me that each day in history, each day in any individual's life is full of divine opportunities. He showed me that God has a plan for us each day of our lives. If we come into agreement with his plan and obey him, then the following pages of the book will show the fruit of our obedience. Likewise, if we don't agree with or obey his plan, then the following pages will show the fruit of our disobedience.

Consider the decision that Adam and Eve made one particular day. They chose to listen to the voice of the enemy instead of the truth of God. And that one act of disobedience has affected every human being that has ever lived on the face of the earth. Every person on the earth has been born with a sinful nature because of their one decision.

> Romans 5:12–14:
>
> Therefore, just as sin entered the world through one man, and death through sin, and in this way death came to all men, because all sinned—
>
> For before the law was given, sin was in the world. But sin is not taken into account when there is no law.
>
> Nevertheless, death reigned from the time of Adam to the time of Moses, even over those who did not sin by breaking a command, as did Adam, who was a pattern of the one to come.

God had told Abraham that he was going to have a son and that through him his descendants would be as numerous as the stars of the sky (Genesis 15:1–5). Abraham believed God, but one day he decided to try to help God out. He decided to have a child through Hagar, one of his wife's servants, and Ishmael was born.

Fourteen years later, God fulfilled his promise to Abraham, and Isaac was born through Sarah, Abraham's wife. The descendants of Ishmael now occupy the Arab nations of the Middle East. The descendants of Isaac are now the nation of Israel and the Jewish people around the world. We all know the strife that exists between the Arabs and Jews. Once again, the decision that Abraham made thousands of years ago is still affecting us today.

On the positive side, consider the decision that Jesus made to obey the Father, and give his life as a sacrifice for the sins of the entire world. His one act of obedience made it possible for all men to be saved and come out from under the curse of the law (Romans 5:15–21). We need to realize how important the decisions we make every day are. They could affect people for the rest of eternity.

Jesus also spoke to me about predestination. Some people believe that God has predetermined every day of our lives. They believe that our lives have been preprogrammed by God and that we have no say in the matter. But what Jesus showed me is that God foreknew the decisions we all would make each day, and what is recorded in his books is the account of our lives based on his foreknowledge.

Again, if we choose to obey him, then the books would record the fruit of our obedience. But if we choose to disobey him, the books would record that fruit also. Our decisions of obedience and disobedience have been prerecorded based on God's foreknowledge of the decisions we would make.

> Romans 8:29: For those God foreknew he also predestined to be conformed to the likeness of his Son, that he might be the firstborn among many brothers.

> Psalm 139:16: All the days ordained for me were written in your book before one of them came to be.

People have used these verses and others to form their opinions about predestination. But again, if God predetermined our lives, then we would have no free will, and we would have no choices to make in our lives. This is not the case.

God offers salvation to all people, but each person must make a decision to receive it by faith. He offers life and blessings in every area of our lives. He has made healing from physical afflictions and deliverance from the power of the enemy possible, but only those who choose to believe it by faith receive the benefits of his promises.

Jesus allowed me to turn back in the pages of the book and see how some of the events of the past came about. Though God had certain plans and destinies for people and for the earth, he chose to give people a free will. He chose to give them a choice of whether or not they would follow and obey him. Many of the things that happened in the past were not God's will for the earth. But they were caused when people chose to listen to the lies of the enemy instead of the truth of God.

In reality, the enemy has no authority on the earth. The only way he gains it is when people come into agreement with his lies. He is then empowered to bring about the very lies that people believe.

I pray that your eyes would be open to see the deception of the enemy. I pray that you would realize how your decisions today affect future generations and that you would choose to obey God's plan for your life.

Chapter 5
The Courts of Heaven

While in intercession one day, I was caught up in the Spirit and taken up into the third heaven. I found myself standing in front of the very throne of God. Jesus appeared beside me as we were standing in front of the throne. The Father, who was seated on his throne, smiled at me as though he was pleased to see me.

The Father told me to have a seat and then disappeared from my sight. When I turned around, I was astonished to see that I was standing in what appeared to be a courtroom. There was a long aisle down the middle of the courtroom. Seated on one side of the aisle were demons, powers, and principalities. They were a nasty-looking bunch, who appeared to me in bodily form. On the other side of the aisle, many angels and many of the saints who had gone on before us were seated. I decided to sit with the angels and saints. There was one open seat in the front row next to Jesus, so I figured it had been reserved for me.

Then the angel that I've come to recognize as Gabriel the archangel, because of his trumpet and his size, stood up and said, "All rise." Everyone in the courtroom stood as God the Father entered the room and sat down on his throne. There was such a sense of awe and reverence as he entered the room, even from the demonic side. I sensed that "no bull" would be allowed in this courtroom.

On trial that day was a city of the world that I had been interceding for, whose name I will not mention. And in particular on trial were the Christian leaders of that city. The prosecuting attorney was the main principality in control over that city. He was very professional in the way he looked and went about his business.

In his opening remarks, the prosecuting attorney made many accusations against the leaders of that city. He charged them with lust, pornography, sexual sins, adultery, pride, greed, manipulation, being poor shepherds, selfish ambitions, disobedience to the word of God, and on and on and on. He said he would call forth eyewitnesses and give evidence as to the validity of these charges. He closed his opening statements with a demand for justice. He said that these leaders deserved to be punished for what they had done.

One by one the prosecuting attorney called forth witnesses from the demonic crowd, who gave testimony of what they had seen these leaders do. He would ask them questions concerning their testimony. They would give account, including names, dates, activities, and sins involved. They would give names of people that had been wounded by the actions of these leaders.

After each testimony, God the Father would turn to an angel seated near the throne and ask if these things were true. The angel would then look in a book and declare that yes indeed, on such and such a date, at such and such a time, the person in question had actually performed the deed mentioned.

Sidebar: every action we make on this earth is being recorded in books by angels in heaven. I was amazed that these demons were not making false accusations. Everything that they were accusing people of was true. It was depressing.

One by one various demons gave testimony and made accusations against the leaders of the city. Each accusation was verified by the recordings in the book. This went on for what seemed to be hours. It was very difficult for me not to develop an attitude myself against the leaders of that city. I was appalled at what I was hearing.

Then the prosecuting attorney gave his closing argument. He declared that every accusation and charge that had been given was verified to be true. He declared that as

Christian leaders, these people should have known better. He demanded that they be punished to the full extent of the law.

The courtroom was deathly silent as everyone there knew that indeed these things were true, and these leaders deserved what they had coming to them. There was a sense of doom and destruction. I was curious to see how God would respond.

Father God then asked, "Who will speak for the defense?" Jesus calmly stood up and said he would. An overwhelming feeling of love, and grace, and mercy suddenly filled the courtroom. Despair turned to hope. The doom and gloom feeling that had previously filled the courtroom suddenly dissipated.

Jesus then began to speak. He said, "I do not deny the validity of any of these charges. We all acknowledge the truth of these claims. I also realize that these leaders will have to give an account to you one day for their actions, but …"

Then he took off his robe so that the stripes on his back could be seen. He held out his hands and feet to reveal the nail scars. He pulled back his hair to show the holes in his scalp from the crown of thorns. Every bruise from every blow that had been dealt to him could be seen on his body. It was a very sobering moment for me.

As I looked at the wounds on his back and body, I noticed that all of the sins the leaders of that city had been accused of were written within his wounds. I also saw the names of sicknesses and diseases within his wounds. I saw fear, depression, rejection, and many other emotional wounds that we deal with written there.

Then Jesus said, "Father, I have already been punished to the full extent of the law on behalf of these leaders. I already paid the full penalty for their sins. I ask that these charges be dropped immediately and that these leaders be declared holy and blameless in your sight."

I began to weep as a revelation of what just happened came to me concerning my own sins. I was completely overwhelmed by the love of God in Christ. I was overcome by mercy. Though all of us deserve to be punished to the full extent of the law, Jesus already took the punishment on our behalf. He took it all, and we get none! None!

Did you get that? He took it all, and we get none! Hallelujah!

God the Father then pronounced his verdict. "Not guilty on all accounts." All of the angels and saints in the room jumped to their feet and began praising and worshiping God. I was still completely overwhelmed but tried my best to join them in worshiping such an awesome God and Savior. The demons and prosecuting attorney left the courtroom in disgust.

This trial had now turned into a party of rejoicing over the goodness of God. Wine was poured and bread was passed out to all of the saints in the room, including me. We lifted our glasses in unison and gave a toast to Jesus our Savior. Tears filled the eyes of all who were there as we realized the awesomeness of our God! Even those who had been there for many years were completely overwhelmed again by the love of God.

I know that many people, even those in the church, have a hard time accepting this truth. Many believe that God is punishing them for their sins. Many believe that God is punishing America and the other nations of the world for their sins. Many prophesy judgment. But what does scripture say?

> John 12:47–48:
>
> As for the person who hears my words but does not keep them, I do not judge him. For I did not come to judge the world, but to save it.
>
> There is a judge for the one who rejects me and does not accept my words; that very word which I spoke will condemn him at the last day.

Jesus said he did not come to judge the world but to save it. He is not even judging those who know his Word but still don't keep it. Ultimately, the only people who will face his judgment are those who reject him. They will be judged at the end. Consider Paul's words to the Romans and Corinthians.

Romans 4:7–8:

Blessed are they whose transgressions are forgiven, whose sins are covered.

Blessed is the man whose sin the Lord will never count against him.

2 Corinthians 5:19–21:

Therefore, if anyone is in Christ, he is a new creation; the old has gone, the new has come!

All this is from God, who reconciled us to himself through Christ and gave us the ministry of reconciliation:

That God was reconciling the world to himself in Christ, not counting men's sins against them.

For those who are in Christ, God is not counting their sins against them. He is never going to count their sins against them. This is the good news of the gospel. This is the superior covenant under which we now live.

Jesus himself said in Matthew 24 that the nations would be judged when the Son of Man comes in his glory. He has not yet come in his glory, so nations are not yet being judged.

Part of the problem is that many people have an inferior revelation of God. And because they have an inferior revelation of God, they make wrong judgments about God and his ways. They often draw incorrect conclusions about God based on God's dealings with people under the Old Covenant. We are no longer under the Old Covenant, but the new one.

I do not feel led to address this issue any further in this book, but God willing, I will address it in detail in my next book.

My prayer is that you will receive a revelation about everything that Jesus accomplished for you on the cross when he took upon himself all of your punishment so that you would get none.

Chapter 6
Demonic Strategy Meeting

The following vision occurred on February 14, 2006.

I was lying in bed praying, about to go to sleep for the night, when Jesus appeared to me in a vision and told me to come with him. Suddenly we were in what seemed to be some type of boardroom, where the enemy was about to have a strategic meeting on how to destroy me.

A large table was in the middle of the room with about a dozen chairs around it. There was also a dry erase board, a video projector, and a screen. A demon of higher rank, perhaps a principality, who I figured was the leader of this meeting, was looking over some papers he had pulled from his briefcase.

Demonic spirits began to arrive and take their place around the table. They were all dressed like businessmen and acted in a very professional manner. They were very serious about what they were about to do. I noticed that as each one sat down, a name would appear on the back of the chair that showed me what each demon represented: death, poverty, rage, discouragement, rejection, and so forth.

The purpose of this meeting was for each demon to report on the progress made against me and to discuss future attempts to destroy me through their evil schemes. The Apostle Paul wrote in 2 Corinthians that he was not unaware of the devil's schemes.

The devil and all his demonic forces are constantly plotting against us in order to steal from, kill, and destroy us. This is the battle we face each day. Whether we believe it or not, it is happening. Many people are destroyed every day because they don't realize the battle they are in.

Remember how I discussed earlier in this book the reality of both the physical and spiritual realm. In the physical realm, this battle may manifest in the form of sickness or disease. But in the spiritual realm, it may actually be demonic forces that are bringing these things upon us through our agreement with their lies.

The meeting was called to order by the leader, who opened it by stating that once again they had failed in their attempt to take my life. There was a sigh of disgust from all of the other demons when he shared that. The leader then asked the spirit of death to give a full report on what had taken place.

The spirit of death then stood up and, with a scowl on his face, began to tell the others about his latest attempt to end my life. He said that he couldn't believe that I had survived this attempt. He said that my neck should have been broken, and I should have died, or at the very least I should have been paralyzed for life. There was no way I should have survived that fall, or so he claimed.

The leader then requested that the video be shown. They showed a video of an accident I had been involved in a few days earlier at work. I was riding on the tailgate of a pickup at about 20 miles per hour when the two supports that hold the tailgate broke.

The tailgate tipped down, and I fell to the pavement, landing on the back of my neck and head with all of my 250 pounds of weight coming down upon me. I remember thinking as I hit the ground that this might be it for me; I might go to be with the Lord at this very moment. My head and neck hit the ground with tremendous force, and then I began to tumble down the road backward, toppling end over end. After a few seconds, I finally came to a stop, not knowing if I was dead or alive. After lying there for a few moments, I stood and began to check myself out to see what injuries I might have.

I was bleeding from a cut on the back of my head, and I also had some cuts and scrapes on my arms and legs, but all in all I was just happy to be alive. My neck was also very sore but seemed to be intact. My coworkers who were driving the truck finally realized that I had fallen off and came back to help me. They wanted to take me to the hospital, but I refused.

The demon of death played that video over and over. He kept saying there was no way I could have survived that fall. I was shocked myself that I had survived after watching the video. All of the other demons were very upset that I had lived and were cursing and swearing at me and calling me hideous names.

Then they showed another video from a few years earlier when I had wrecked my truck into the back of a parked car at 65 miles per hour and didn't even get hurt. I wasn't wearing a seatbelt at the time either. They also showed other video clips of various attempts that they had made to take my life, but each time they had failed. They were really frustrated with me.

It became very clear to me as they were showing these videos just how often God had protected my life from the traps of the enemy. I kept looking at Jesus, somewhat in disbelief at what I was watching and somewhat amazed at all he had done to protect me. I was falling more and more in love with him with each passing moment. I was so grateful to God that he is alive and active in my life.

When the spirit of death was finished, the leader asked the spirit of poverty to speak next. The spirit of poverty began by saying that once again he had come so close to getting me to give up, but God had come through for me and renewed my faith. I had been working out of town and had the added expenses of apartment rent, groceries, gas, electric bills, etc. Our finances were a wreck, and we were getting further and further in debt. I didn't know what to do but kept crying out to God for help.

One weekend, while at a revival service, God directed the speaker to take up an offering for me. He didn't know anything about my financial situation. He asked people to sow into my life and ministry. They collected about $600 for me, which wasn't nearly enough to get me out of the jam I was in, but it was enough to restore my faith in God.

Then my wife had a job working as a medical secretary dropped in her lap. Once again, God was providing and showing his faithfulness.

Later, while ministering in Maryland one weekend, God had directed me to give all the money in my ministry account to a man in attendance. It was difficult for my flesh, but I wrote out a check for the balance of my ministry account, which was only about $550 at the time. But when money is as tight as it was for us at the time, it was a big deal.

About a week later, I received a check for $5,000 from a man in Maryland. He said God had directed him to do so. A few months later, he sent me another check for the same amount and also bought me a laptop computer. Isn't God faithful?

All of these things lifted my faith and renewed my hope in God. Discouragement fled, and poverty was broken, instead of me. The demons were once again very upset over all of this.

The spirit of rage was next to speak. He was a very loud and angry one. He was working closely with another demon called sleep deprivation to try to destroy my testimony in front of my coworkers. They knew that when I get really tired, I tend to lose my temper much more quickly. So sleep deprivation would torment through the night to keep me from getting the rest I needed.

Then the spirit of rage would cause things to go wrong during the day in an attempt to get me frustrated and get me to lose my temper. He would also try to stir up feelings of rage within me to get me to fly off the handle and ruin my testimony. For the most part, they were unsuccessful, but they did get me once in a while.

One by one each of the demons around the table took turns showing video clips and speaking about how they had tried to destroy me. There was rejection, division, confusion, lust, and others. I was horrified as I watched the videos of all their scheming against me and my family.

And at times they would work together to try to destroy the relationship between me and my wife. There were times when they came close to getting us to separate, but ultimately every attempt had failed. They had pitted the weaknesses in me against the weaknesses in her. Our love and faith were severely tested but proved to be genuine.

God had set me free from many of the rejection and lust issues that previously had me struggling. He had given me revelation of his great love for me. He was teaching me how to love my wife as Christ loved the church. All of this helped me to overcome these demonic attempts to destroy me.

All of the demons had finished reporting, and I thought the meeting was about to end. But the leader announced that he had invited a special guest tonight. He called in a loud voice toward the door, and a very evil-looking spirit came through the door looking extremely upset. He was a demon of cancer. The leader told him he was free to speak.

The spirit of cancer began pleading with the other demons to do something radical to stop me, because I was now focusing my attention toward him. He was cursing and trying to motivate them against me. He wanted them to destroy me before I destroyed him.

Let me state that I believe it is God's will for all people to be saved, healed, and delivered from the power of the enemy. When Jesus died on the cross, he not only bore our sins, but he also carried our infirmities and our sorrows. He died so that we could be made completely whole—body, soul, and spirit (Isaiah 53).

God spoke to me once and said that if you really want to know God's will concerning any issue, just look at Jesus. Consider the words of the writer of Hebrews.

> Hebrews 1:3: The Son is the radiance of God's glory and the exact representation of his being.

Jesus is the exact representation of the Father. He is not a shadow of him. He is not a cheap imitation of him. He is the exact representation of the Father. Listen to the words of Jesus himself concerning this issue.

> John 10:30: I and the Father are one.

> John 14:9: Anyone who has seen me has seen the Father.

> John 6:38: For I have come down from heaven not to do my will but to do the will of him who sent me.

> John 5:19: Jesus gave them this answer: "I tell you the truth, the Son can do nothing by himself; he can do only what he sees his Father doing, because whatever the Father does the Son also does."

In light of these scriptures, and many others that I did not mention, I want you to consider this. Jesus healed all the sick that came to him. In doing so, he was doing exactly what he saw the Father doing, and he was doing his

Father's will. What does that say to us about the Father's will concerning healing? Again, I believe it is God's will for all to be healed.

There are many people who believe that God put sickness or disease on them to teach them a lesson about something. If God put that on you, and then Jesus came along and healed you, would he be doing what he saw his Father doing? No, he would be doing the exact opposite.

Sickness and disease are the result of living in a fallen world where the effects of sin have taken their toll on the earth and on mankind. They are also the work of the devil. But they do not come from God.

Now, let's get back to the vision. There are three diseases that God has really put on my heart to go after. I encounter people nearly every day of my life who have one or more of these diseases. They are cancer, diabetes, and arthritis. Because of my belief in the will of God concerning healing, and because of the desire that God put in my heart to destroy these diseases, I love to pray for anyone I encounter who is suffering from them.

I have seen many people healed of various forms of these diseases. That is why I believe this spirit of cancer was trying so hard to get these other demons to destroy me, before I destroyed him.

All of the other demons agreed that I must be stopped. But to date, all of their efforts to destroy me have failed.

Thank God for his protection! The spirit of cancer then left the room in a fit of rage. The other demons just sat there in silence.

The leader then told everyone to do some brainstorming to see if they could come up with some scheme that might work against me. He said they would meet again shortly to see if anyone had come up with anything. He also told everyone to continue to harass me as best they could. It was very scary listening to and seeing all of this.

I turned to look at Jesus to see what he was thinking about all of this. He just smiled at me with a look that said, "Don't worry. I got your back."

Words cannot properly express my love and gratitude for Jesus because of all he has done and continues to do on my behalf. He is such an awesome God!!

I pray you would gain some understanding of the war that you are in against the powers of darkness, and that you would get an even greater understanding of how God protects you because of his great love for you!

Chapter 7
Angels

Whether we realize it or not, angels are a big part of kingdom reality and play a significant role in our lives on a regular basis. A quick study of scripture reveals angelic involvement in people's lives from Genesis to Revelation. Because of the gift that God has given me, I see angels on a regular basis and have had numerous encounters with them over the years.

Many times during services or meetings, I know what God wants to do because of what I see the angels doing. I am constantly asking him to show me what he is doing so that I can come into alignment with his plans. Jesus only did what he saw his Father doing. We should do likewise. And many times God shows me what he is doing by allowing me to see what the angels are doing.

Jesus himself had said in the book of John that we would see heaven open and angels ascending and descending.

The angels actually work with us to bring forth the will of the Father on the earth. In a sense, they are colaborers with us. Their desire and ministry is to serve God and help accomplish his plans and purposes for our lives.

> Hebrews 1:7: In speaking of the angels he says, "He makes his angels winds, his servants flames of fire."

> Hebrews 1:14: Are not all angels ministering spirits sent to serve those who will inherit salvation?

On one of my encounters, I actually saw God the Father assigning angels to work with his people. The size and seriousness of the mission determined the number of angels that were assigned to that person or group and the level of authority that those angels carried. The level of control that the enemy had over an area or people also helped determine angelic assignments.

Through my study of scripture and various encounters with angels, I have come to the following conclusions. Angels get excited about working with mankind to serve God. When God assigns them to a person or group, those who are typically obedient to the Father and who are kingdom-minded, the angels get all fired up and can't wait for the mission to begin. Likewise, when God assigns angels to individuals or groups of people who aren't kingdom-minded and who typically don't obey the Father, they become sad.

Angels love God. They love to serve God. They love to worship God. They love to fight against the enemy. They love to be a part of what God is doing on the earth through his people. They love to minister to people. They love to protect people. They love to deliver messages to God's people directly from the throne of God.

In my experiences over the years, I have observed nine types of angels, which I determined by the type of ministry that they carried out. They are: worshiping angels, guardian angels, messenger angels, warrior angels, ministry angels, worker angels, recording angels, escort angels, and harvesting angels.

Sometimes they radiate light, sometimes not. Sometimes they have wings, sometimes not. Sometimes I can tell the authority that an angel carries by its size. The Archangels Michael and Gabriel are two of the largest angels that I have seen. They always appear larger than the angels around them and have reached heights of forty to fifty feet!

Occasionally, I am frightened when I first see them. And typically the first thing they say to me is the same comment that they made to people in the Bible, "Fear not."

After I realize who they are, a great peace often comes over me. This is followed by an overwhelming sense of expectancy, as I know that something wonderful is about to happen.

I would like to share a few of my experiences with each of these types of angels.

Worshiping Angels

> Revelation 5:11–14:

> Then I looked and heard the voice of many angels, numbering thousands upon thousands, and ten thousand times ten thousand. They encircled the throne and the living creatures and the elders.

> In a loud voice they sang: "Worthy is the Lamb, who was slain, to receive power and wealth and wisdom and strength and honor and glory and praise!"

> Then I heard every creature in heaven and on earth and under the earth and on the sea, and all that is in them, singing: "To him who sits on the throne and to the Lamb be praise and honor and glory and power, for ever and ever!"

> The four living creatures said, "Amen," and the elders fell down and worshiped

> Revelation 7:11–12

> All the angels were standing around the throne and around the elders and the four living creatures. They fell down on their faces before the throne and worshiped God,

Saying: "Amen! Praise and glory and wisdom
and thanks and honor and power and strength
be to our God for ever and ever. Amen!"

There are thousands upon thousands of angels whose chief duty or assignment is to worship God day and night. Many of them do this directly around the throne of God. Others have been assigned to worship God from the earth along with us.

In almost every worship service that I have been involved in, where people are truly worshiping God in spirit and in truth, I see angels worshiping with us. There are usually a number of them playing various instruments, others who are singing, some waving flags, others dancing, and still others bowing before the Lord and making these simple but powerful declarations, "Holy, Holy, Holy, is the Lord God Almighty" and "Worthy is the Lamb who was slain."

And anywhere true worship is being lifted up, the presence of God comes. And not only does his presence come, but God actually inhabits, or establishes his throne, wherever he is truly praised. And the worshiping angels follow him and worship him wherever he goes. See Psalm 22:3.

I have participated in times of worship where the number of voices actually singing worship to God far outnumbered the number of people who were present at the service. I believe I heard audibly the voices of the angels joining with us in worship. I have heard instruments playing that weren't part of the worship team's repertoire. I have seen angels playing harps, trumpets, drums, and other instruments. All of this really enhances our times of worship and attracts the presence of God.

Angels love to worship their Creator. And they really enjoy worshiping alongside other created beings. They love to join with us in worship of the One who is truly worthy.

Guardian Angels

Everywhere I go, I see angels who have been assigned to guard or protect the people that God has assigned them to. I have even seen my own guardian angel(s) on several occasions.

> Psalm 91:11: For he will command his angels concerning you to guard you in all your ways.

Once when I was a child, an angel appeared to me as a man and carried me off of the middle of the road just seconds before I would have been hit by an oncoming car. Then he disappeared into thin air. I wasn't even a believer at the time.

I was involved in a traffic accident where I slammed into the back of a parked car that had just wrecked, while I was traveling at 65 mph. I should have been killed or seriously injured, but just prior to hitting the car, I saw an angel lie across my bumper, forming a cushion between my vehicle and the other one.

Everything happened so fast that I didn't have time to realize that we were being saved by this angel, but the realization hit me afterward and I was again grateful to God for sending this angel. I didn't receive one scratch, and neither did my brother, who was riding with me. Even the police officers who came to the scene couldn't believe that we weren't killed or seriously injured.

I had worked as an electrician in the construction industry for about twenty years. Just prior to quitting my job to be in full-time ministry, the enemy tried to take my life on three occasions. On one of them, two angels literally picked me up and carried me to safety.

I was working on a prison in Camp Hill, Pennsylvania. It was nearing the end of the project, so we were just doing some finish wiring and connections. I was working above the metal ceiling in a cellblock making final connections to the fire alarm system. It was about eighteen feet from the concrete floor up to the ceiling.

To get above this ceiling, I had set up scaffolding and then was climbing up a six-foot ladder on top of the scaffolding to crawl up through a two-foot by two-foot access panel in the ceiling. I had locked the wheels on the scaffolding in place so it wouldn't move as I crawled up the ladder and through the opening.

I had to come down from the ceiling to attend a meeting. When I returned from the meeting, the scaffolding was still in the same place, so I assumed that no one had used it, and the wheels were still locked. I actually never gave it a thought to even check it. However, as I was climbing up the ladder and through the access panel, the scaffolding began to roll out from under me.

Before I even had time to think or react, the scaffolding had rolled completely out from under me, and the ladder went crashing to the floor. I fell back down through the access panel but managed to grab on to the edge of the metal ceiling by the tips of my fingers. I now found myself dangling by my fingertips eighteen feet above a concrete floor.

I tried to pull myself up, but my fingers weren't strong enough, and I didn't have enough grip on the edge of the ceiling. I tried yelling to two of my coworkers who were working on the other side of the building, but they couldn't hear me. I cried out to God to help me, realizing I only had a few seconds left before I fell.

At best, I would have broken some or many bones and would have been seriously injured. At worst, this might have been the end of my life.

A metal landing where a set of steps came up to the second floor was about eight feet from me. But there was no way for me to reach for it. I managed to swing my feet over and touch the top rail of the landing, but that didn't do me any good.

By now the metal ceiling was beginning to cut through my fingertips and all of my fingers were bleeding. I was actually trying to figure out how to land as I fell that would afford me the best chance of surviving, and then I was going to let go, having no hope of reaching safety.

All of a sudden, two angels picked me up and carried me over to the landing. *Holy Wow*!! I spent the next twenty to thirty minutes worshiping God. Then I went over to the other side of the building and told my coworkers what had happened. I showed them my bleeding fingers. They were astonished, but I wasn't sure if they believed me.

So we took a tape measure and measured from the edge of the access panel to the top rail of the landing. It measured exactly eight feet. I am six feet one, and standing on the tip of my toes, I can barely touch an eight-foot ceiling. But there was no way I could reach that railing, especially considering that my hands were hanging from the access panel, not reaching for the railing. My coworkers now believed.

These are just a few of the experiences that I have had with guardian angels over the years. Whether you see them or not, they are there. And they are constantly working to protect us from the schemes of the enemy. Praise God!

Messenger Angels

Daniel 9:20–22:

While I was speaking and praying, confessing my sin and the sin of my people Israel and making my request to the LORD my God for his holy hill—

While I was still in prayer, Gabriel, the man I had seen in the earlier vision, came to me in swift flight about the time of the evening sacrifice.

He instructed me and said to me, "Daniel, I have now come to give you insight and understanding."

Luke 1:26–37:

In the sixth month, God sent the angel Gabriel to Nazareth, a town in Galilee,

To a virgin pledged to be married to a man named Joseph, a descendant of David. The virgin's name was Mary.

The angel went to her and said, "Greetings, you who are highly favored! The Lord is with you."

Mary was greatly troubled at his words and wondered what kind of greeting this might be.

But the angel said to her, "Do not be afraid, Mary, you have found favor with God.

"You will be with child and give birth to a son, and you are to give him the name Jesus.

"He will be great and will be called the Son of the Most High. The Lord God will give him the throne of his father David,

"And he will reign over the house of Jacob forever; his kingdom will never end."

"How will this be," Mary asked the angel, "since I am a virgin?"

The angel answered, "The Holy Spirit will come upon you, and the power of the Most High will overshadow you. So the holy one to be born will be called the Son of God.

"Even Elizabeth your relative is going to have a child in her old age, and she who was said to be barren is in her sixth month.

"For nothing is impossible with God."

Notice Mary's response to Gabriel's message. She put complete faith and trust in what the angel had told her. How many of us would do that?

Luke 1:38: "I am the Lord's servant," Mary answered. "May it be to me as you have said." Then the angel left her.

Numerous times over the years angels have appeared to me and delivered messages to me directly from the throne of God. Why does God speak to us directly sometimes, but at other times he sends angels to speak to us? I don't know, except that he is God and can reveal himself to us any way he wants.

But the fact remains that God does send angels to speak to us at times. They can deliver words of knowledge about past events. They can communicate the present will of God to us. They can reveal future events to us. They can communicate the heart of God to us. They can give us revelation about ourselves, others, or even God at times. They can reveal to us anything that God wants us to know.

In the next chapter, I will share an encounter I had with an angel that I was allowed to call Kathy. To me, she was both a messenger angel but also a ministering angel. But for now, I will at least share this encounter.

An angel appeared beside my bed one time while I was sleeping. I was startled awake by a loud trumpet blast and awoke to see this large angel beside me. I believe it was Gabriel. Don't ask me how I know that, I just do. Many times during these encounters we receive revelation, an inner knowing, without anybody actually speaking to us.

I, of course, was afraid at first. But after calming down, I noticed the angel was holding a scroll in his hand. I asked him if he had a message for me. He said yes, and then proceeded to open the scroll and read to me what was written on it.

He spoke in an angelic tongue that I could not understand with my physical hearing, but I understood every word he said in my heart and spirit. He revealed to me how God saw me and many things about God's will and plans for my life. I felt such freedom as he spoke, as if things were breaking off of me and lifting off of me.

Jesus said in John 8 that we would know the truth, and the truth would set us free. As the angel spoke truth into my life, I received more and more freedom. Issues of rejection and insecurity that I had dealt with for many years were lifted off of me, all through a message delivered to me by an angel. Certain aspects of God's will for my life were also made known to me.

Warrior Angels

Ephesians 6:12: For our struggle is not against flesh and blood, but against the rulers, against the authorities, against the powers of this dark world and against the spiritual forces of evil in the heavenly realms.

Revelation 12:7–9:

> And there was war in heaven. Michael and his angels fought against the dragon, and the dragon and his angels fought back.
>
> But he was not strong enough, and they lost their place in heaven.
>
> The great dragon was hurled down—that ancient serpent called the devil, or Satan, who leads the whole world astray. He was hurled to the earth, and his angels with him.

Satan and his angels were hurled down to the earth, where they now set out to kill, steal, and destroy mankind. Satan hates God, and since mankind is the only being created in God's image, Satan also hates us. And he is out to destroy us at all costs.

God has given us complete authority over the enemy, but unfortunately we surrender that authority to him anytime we come into agreement with his lies. We are in a constant struggle in our minds between the lies of the enemy and the truth of God. The enemy is empowered by our agreement, and we actually surrender authority on the earth and in the heavenly realms to him.

Because of this, there is a constant, ongoing battle in the heavenly realms between the angels and Satan and his demons. Angels are assigned by God to war against the enemy on our behalf. These assignments are directly related to the work of the church. Anywhere true believers are doing the work of the kingdom, angels work with us and do warfare on our behalf.

Something that I have noticed over the years is that warfare activity by the angels is often, but not always, related to the amount of intercession being done by the saints. As we lift up others before the throne of grace and stand in the gap on their behalf, God releases angels to make war against the evil spirits that are oppressing people.

I do not have a complete understanding of these things, and I have much more to learn in this area, but it seems that the more we come into alignment with God's will, plans, and purposes, the greater authority and power that we and the angels are able to exercise over the enemy. Remember in chapter 3 of this book how Michael was empowered to cut off the serpent's head when we came into alignment with God?

A number of years ago, during a presidential election year, the Lord had given me a couple of visions concerning the outcome of the elections. He showed me what would happen to this country if a certain individual was elected. I am not here to discuss politics. I am neither Republican nor Democrat. I vote according to how the Spirit of God leads me.

But I was truly concerned about the future of this country. I began heavily interceding for this nation, asking the Lord to show me how to pray. God showed me a vision of a principality that was working behind the scenes to promote this particular candidate and to bring about the destruction of this nation. I really didn't know what to do, but I began rebuking that principality and asking God to deal with it.

One night while we were interceding at the church, Michael, the archangel, rode into the church on a white horse. He was dressed in full body armor, carrying a shield and a huge sword. He looked at me and asked, "What is it you want me to do for you?"

After the shock of his question wore off, I asked him if he could defeat that principality. He nodded his head yes. So I said, "Then go." He then turned and rode up through the ceiling of the church and headed toward Florida. Don't ask me how I knew that, I just did. I sensed that Florida would be critical to the upcoming election.

After just a few minutes, Michael returned to the church. He drew his sword, and I could see that it was covered in "spiritual blood," and I knew that Michael had won the battle. He took a cloth and wiped the blood from his sword. As he turned to leave, I thanked him. Once again, he nodded his head and then rode off into the heavens.

Ministry Angels

Remember the scripture from Hebrews 1:14 that said that all angels are ministering spirits sent to serve those who will inherit salvation. Many times over the years, I have seen ministering angels show up during services, prayer meetings, conferences, etc. They typically appear to me as angels with gifts wrapped up with bows like Christmas presents.

Back in 2004, I was on a mission trip to Brazil with Randy Clark and Global Awakening. We were ministering in a large gymnasium. We noticed that in one section of seating, people were falling out under the power of God. Randy asked if anyone could see what was going on over there. When I looked over, I saw a shaft of light coming down from heaven, representing an open heaven. The shaft was about twenty feet round, and everyone seated in that area was falling out.

Suddenly, I saw angels beginning to descend and ascend in that open heaven. The ones coming down were bringing gifts and giving them to people. Then they would go back up to heaven to get more. They were bringing spiritual gifts to people. They were bringing gifts of salvation, healing, and deliverance for people. When I shared this with Randy, he began to cooperate with the angels and the Holy Spirit and all heaven broke loose.

On another occasion I was ministering to a small group of people, and I saw some ministering angels come in bearing gifts. I began to pray for people and released the angels to give away their gifts. One angel gave a gift to a woman, and her hands began to ooze with oil. She had received a gift of healing, and every time her hands manifest the oil, she knows that God wants to heal someone.

These angels will also minister to us during times of great trial or hardship. Consider how they ministered to Jesus just after his time of fasting and temptation in the desert and also in the Garden of Gethsemane.

> Matthew 4:11: Then the devil left him, and angels came and attended him.

> Luke 22:43: An angel from heaven appeared to him and strengthened him.

Worker Angels

> Psalm 103:20–21:

> Praise the LORD, you his angels, you mighty ones who do his bidding, who obey his word.

> Praise the LORD, all his heavenly hosts, you his servants who do his will.

For lack of a better term, I will call the next group of angels that I want to cover worker angels. I had thought about some other names, such as gathering angels or servant angels, but worker seems to be the best fit, at least for now.

Worker angels simply do what their name denotes, they work. They are like the worker bees of a bee colony. Let me share a couple of quick examples.

My family owns a piece of property of about seventy-five acres. It was previously owned by my dad and two uncles as part of a farm that they owned together. They had been out of the farming business for many years, and my uncles wanted to sell the land.

My mom, Cinda, was considering whether to buy my uncles' share of the land. She had asked all of us if we could see any reason to keep the land. She was also curious about any curses that might be on the land as a result of all the fighting that took place over the years on that property, mostly between family members.

I had a vision of one day building an apostolic training and healing center on that land. So my mom decided to buy the land. Then we decided to pray over the land and break any generational curses that might remain there. We also blessed the land.

I later had another vision of worker angels coming and preparing the land for God's purposes. First they plowed the entire property. Then they went through and picked out all of the rocks, removed some old, rotten stumps, and removed all of the weeds. Then they seeded and fertilized the entire property, and within minutes a beautiful green field appeared. I knew that the land was now ready to be used for building the kingdom.

At other times, I have seen worker angels show up and begin construction in the spiritual realm, which I know meant that God was about to build another part of his kingdom there. I have seen them bring all kinds of supplies to areas in order to begin a new work for the Lord in an area. I have seen them do remodeling work in churches and I knew that God was about to do a new thing there.

I watched them build an embassy on the property of one of my good friends in Maryland. Now the embassy is occupied by other angels, who are busy carrying out the Father's orders from there. And all of this is directly related to the intercession that is made on that property by my friend. There are things happening in the spiritual realm all over the world as a result of this embassy.

Watching/Recording Angels

> Revelation 20:12: And I saw the dead, great and small, standing before the throne, and books were opened. Another book was opened, which is the book of life. The dead were judged according to what they had done as recorded in the books.

On some of my visits to the heavens, I have seen angels who record in books all of the events that take place on the earth. There are millions of books in heaven that contain detailed accounts of every happening on the earth. Unbelievers could never stand before God and lie about the details of their lives, as every word, thought, event, and circumstance of their lives are being recorded in books by angels.

Many times I have seen angels who just watch what is happening on the earth. Then they report back to God what they have seen and heard. God then instructs them to record their witness in the books so that accurate records are kept on the people and events of the earth.

All of our good works are also being recorded. These are the records that will be used to determine our rewards in heaven. I know at times we get discouraged because it seems that for all of our hard work for the kingdom, we don't see much fruit. But take heart, my friends, nothing you do for his sake goes unrecorded. And one day you will receive your just reward.

Escort Angels

Escort angels have a special assignment from the Lord. The moment a believer passes from this world into the next, these angels escort them into the very throne room of God. To be absent from the body is to be present with the Lord!

> Luke 16:22: The time came when the beggar died and the angels carried him to Abraham's side. The rich man also died and was buried.

Harvesting Angels

> Matthew 13:24–39:
>
> Jesus told them another parable: "The kingdom of heaven is like a man who sowed good seed in his field.

"But while everyone was sleeping, his enemy came and sowed weeds among the wheat, and went away.

"When the wheat sprouted and formed heads, then the weeds also appeared.

"The owner's servants came to him and said, 'Sir, didn't you sow good seed in your field? Where then did the weeds come from?'

"'An enemy did this,' he replied.'" The servants asked him, 'Do you want us to go and pull them up?'

"'No,' he answered, 'because while you are pulling the weeds, you may root up the wheat with them.

"'Let both grow together until the harvest. At that time I will tell the harvesters: First collect the weeds and tie them in bundles to be burned; then gather the wheat and bring it into my barn.'"

He told them another parable: "The kingdom of heaven is like a mustard seed, which a man took and planted in his field.

"Though it is the smallest of all your seeds, yet when it grows, it is the largest of garden plants and becomes a tree, so that the birds of the air come and perch in its branches."

He told them still another parable: "The kingdom of heaven is like yeast that a woman took and mixed into a large amount of flour until it worked all through the dough."

Jesus spoke all these things to the crowd in parables; he did not say anything to them without using a parable.

So was fulfilled what was spoken through the prophet: "I will open my mouth in parables, I will utter things hidden since the creation of the world."

Then he left the crowd and went into the house. His disciples came to him and said, "Explain to us the parable of the weeds in the field."

He answered, "The one who sowed the good seed is the Son of Man.

"The field is the world, and the good seed stands for the sons of the kingdom. The weeds are the sons of the evil one,

"And the enemy who sows them is the devil. The harvest is the end of the age, and the harvesters are angels."

Numerous times over the years, I have seen ripened fruit or grain in the spiritual realm. This typically means that seeds have grown to maturity and are ready to be harvested. I have also seen angels show up with sickles and other instruments that are used to harvest crops. I knew that it was harvest time.

There are seasons in the spiritual realm just as there are seasons in the physical realm. Farmers plant seeds, water them, fertilize them, and then harvest them when they are fully grown and mature. In the same way, we plant seeds in people's lives, water them, fertilize them, and then harvest them in due time. When I see mature fruit, and angels show up with harvesting tools, I know a harvest is near.

This harvest could include the salvation of souls. It could represent many physical or emotional healings are about to take place. It could mean that people have reached a level of maturity and are about to move into kingdom realities. It could mean that God is about to do a mighty work in an area.

But whatever the case, when I see harvesting angels show up, I know that something good is about to happen, and I want to be a part of it.

I pray that you would have faith to believe in how God uses angels, that you might see or somehow feel their presence, and that you might receive all that Father God sends to you through his angels.

Chapter 8
Kathy

I believe that God assigns angels to us at times to work with us to build the kingdom. For instance, in the book of Daniel, the angel that came to bring God's reply to Daniel referred to Michael, the archangel, as Daniel's prince. I believe that God had assigned Michael to Daniel for a season. See Daniel 10.

A couple of years ago, I believe that God assigned an angel to me for a season. Here is the account of that season.

I was scheduled to do a three-day deliverance conference at Crossroads Alliance Church in Ebensburg, Pennsylvania. The night before the conference, I was suddenly startled awake around 3:00 a.m. by something in my bedroom. Standing beside my bed on my wife's side was a woman dressed in a red blouse and blue jeans.

At first I thought it was my wife, and I was about to say to her, "What in the world are you doing?" But then I realized that my wife was still sleeping beside me. I knew then that this was an angel. I asked her what she wanted.

She came over to my side of the bed and told me that she was going to be ministering with me at the conference. She said that she carried a special anointing to break generational curses and that whenever she appeared behind someone at the conference, I was supposed to go to that person and break the generational curses off of his or her life.

I asked her if she had a name. She said that I could call her Kathy. I sensed that Kathy was not her real name, but for the sake of ease, that is what I called her.

I believe that because angels are spirits, they are neither male nor female. However, based on their assignments, they appear to us as male or female. Scripture mentions the archangels Michael and Gabriel. Both of these are male figures, though they are spirits.

The next three nights as I ministered at the conference, Kathy would appear from time to time. I would then go back and break the generational curse off of the person and sometimes also prophesy to him or her. It was a very powerful conference, as I was able to cooperate with this angel. People were crying, and they received much healing and freedom throughout the three nights.

A few months later, I was scheduled to minister at the Rome Christian Center in Rome, New York. Through a unique set of "God circumstances," we found ourselves at the grave site of Daniel Nash on Saturday morning. God had sent us there to redig an ancient well and to tap into that anointing.

Daniel Nash was the chief intercessor for a revivalist named Charles Finney. Nash would go into cities ahead of Finney and petition the throne of God until he got a breakthrough in the spiritual realm. Finney would then show up, and entire cities would receive the Gospel and be saved!

While we were praying at the grave site, my cell phone rang. A woman from New York who was with us, Kelly Flemming, who as of this writing is a student at the Global School of Supernatural Ministry, said that it's probably God calling. When I pulled my cell phone out of my pocket and looked at it, it read, "restricted call." I had never received a restricted call before, nor have I since then. When I answered the phone, this is what I heard.

"Hi, Rick. Don't say anything; just listen. You know who this is. I just wanted to tell you that I will be in church tomorrow to minister with you again. When you see me appear behind someone, go to them, and I will either give you a prophetic word for them or have you minister healing or deliverance to them. I'll see ya tomorrow. Bye."

Incidentally, I later checked my cell phone records, and there was no record of that call.

The next morning, just as she had told me, Kathy appeared numerous times during the service, and I would stop preaching and go and minister to the person she directed me to. She gave me numerous prophetic words for people that were cutting them to the heart. Others were supernaturally healed by the power of God. Some received deliverance from oppression to the enemy. Once again, God performed miraculous signs and wonders!

I was really enjoying working with this angel. It was amazing what God was doing through us. I didn't know how long this would last, but I determined to enjoy every moment that she was here.

A couple of months later, I was ministering at a church in Delaware. Friday afternoon before the evening service, we were sitting in the back of the church eating lunch. When I looked out toward the seats, I saw Kathy sitting there. She motioned with her finger for me to come back to her.

So I went back and sat next to her, and for the next hour she gave me prophetic messages for people who would be coming to service that night. I wrote all of the words down and spoke them over the appropriate people during the service that night. Once again, these words really cut people to the heart. They were greatly strengthened, encouraged, and comforted. Saturday and Sunday services were also very powerful. Many people were touched by the power of God. It was an amazing time in the Lord for those few months.

I only saw Kathy one other time after that, for a brief moment. We didn't speak, but I knew she was with me on that occasion. I do not understand why she was only sent to me for that season of about six months, but I thanked God for the blessing that she was to me and to many others.

Since that time, many other angels have shown up and ministered with me, but I didn't get to speak with them as personally as I did with Kathy. Most of them did not reveal their names to me, and many of them didn't speak to me. They would just show up and begin ministering to people, and I would do my best to cooperate with them.

I even asked God if I had done something wrong that Kathy was no longer with me. He said no. He said he had other assignments for her. Of course, I had to be okay with that, but I do miss Kathy from time to time.

I pray for seasons of extreme angelic blessings to come upon all of your lives!

Chapter 9
The Tree of Life

It was a Sunday evening, and I had just finished ministering at a healing conference in Pennsylvania. I was getting prepared to leave and was talking with some of the people of the church. People were still lying on the floor being ministered to by the Lord. He had done some incredible miracles!

A few of the people decided to pray for me before I left. When they did, I fell under the presence of the Lord. Immediately, I saw Jesus standing up in heaven. He called to me as he had done many times in the past and said, "Come up here." Once again I found myself zooming up through the heavenly realms.

When I arrived there, wherever *there* was, I found myself standing in front of the Tree of Life. So much glory was emanating from it that I could barely stand or breathe. The tree had a gold-like glow all around it. The bark and the leaves of the tree were gold-colored. Little particles of gold glory were shooting off from it like small fireworks. The fruit on the tree was gold-colored with a reddish tint.

The glory of the Lord was overwhelming me. I fell to my knees and bowed with my face to the ground. Then the voice that had called me to come there spoke again. When I looked up at the tree again, I could see the face of Jesus in the tree. The leaves and branches had become the living face of Jesus.

Of course, I thought. Jesus is the tree of life. He called to me to come closer. I crawled on my hands and knees till I was under the tree. Then Jesus said, "Eat my flesh and drink my blood." In my spirit I realized that the leaves of the tree were his flesh and that the fruit of the tree was his blood.

Once again, I cannot explain how I knew this, but when you are in those realms, you know and understand things by the Spirit that you couldn't possibly figure out with your own knowledge.

I plucked a couple of leaves from the tree and began to chew on them. As I did, Jesus spoke to me and said, "The leaves of the trees are for the healing of the nations. Go and heal the nations." When he spoke those words, a surge of power streamed through my body and completely invigorated me.

The leaves tasted bitter to me. I sensed that this greater anointing for healing that I was presently receiving would be bitter to me. It would be bitter in that it would require even more of my time. It would mean even greater responsibility. It would mean bigger devils to confront. Many people say that they want greater anointing, but they don't realize the personal cost that comes with it. I have counted the cost, and am willing to pay the price.

Then I plucked a piece of fruit from the tree and took a bite from it. It was the sweetest and juiciest fruit I have ever eaten. Life surged through my body like a mighty rushing river. Then Jesus spoke and said, "I am the source of all life. Apart from me, there is no life. Those who eat of me shall never hunger or thirst again."

As I continued eating the fruit, wave after wave of life just surged through my body, penetrating even into my soul and spirit. My entire being—body, soul, and spirit—was being refreshed. I have never been more satisfied. I had no lack, nor even want. I was at perfect peace in every fiber of my being.

Jesus completely fulfilled me—my every want, my every need. He satisfied me in every way like I had never been satisfied before. He desires for all of us to come to him and be satisfied. He is the Tree of Life. He is the essence of life itself. He is life.

Those who draw near to him and live intimately with him will experience his life. He will be their source of life. He will be the provision in every area of their lives: spiritually, physically, emotionally, financially, in ministry, in their families, in every relationship. There aren't any areas of life that Jesus, the source of life, cannot touch.

Jesus spoke to me again and said, "The life you are presently experiencing is the life that I desire for all of my body. Most people never come close to experiencing this life. Instead, they live a life of religious obligations without ever really having intimacy and life in me."

I was saddened by his statement. Why do we choose inferior things and inferior relationships when we have the opportunity to be so close to the very creator of the universe? Why do we choose religious activities over true kingdom life? Why do we settle for meaningless religion when we could have a meaningful relationship?

Perhaps the church has misrepresented God to the world, and even to the body, to such a degree that we no longer even know or understand what a real relationship with God is. What if we have drifted so far from the truth that all we have now is a form of godliness but deny the power thereof (2 Timothy 3:5)?

Relationships are something that we experience. And if we aren't experiencing God in our relationship with him, then maybe we really don't have a relationship. Maybe all we have is religion.

Every relationship we have with every person on the earth involves a couple of things. First, it involves two-way communication. There are no relationships apart from communication. Second, it involves experiencing each other's presence. I can't have a relationship with anyone outside of communication and presence. Is it any different with God? How can we claim to have a relationship with him apart from two-way communication and experience of his presence? I'm just saying ...

I pray that the lines of communication between you and God would be completely restored and that you would experience his presence on a regular basis.

Chapter 10
Jesus Is Everything

While in worship at Crossroads Church one day, I entered into a vision. I saw Jesus walking down this street in heaven. On both sides of the street were thousands upon thousands of people who were bowing down to worship Jesus as he passed by. They were weeping and crying and just loving him with all that was within them. Also, thousands of angels were joining in to worship the one who is worthy. I too was overwhelmed with love for this one called Jesus.

When he first appeared, he was in the form of a man, dressed in a white robe with a purple sash draped around him. But as he was walking down the street, he began to appear in many different forms. He first turned into the Lamb that was slain. Then he turned into the Lion of the tribe of Judah. About every eight to ten seconds, he took on a different form, but each form he turned into was one of the names or references to him from the Bible. I was awestruck! I wept and wept in adoration of him.

He was Almighty God but also a Friend who sticks closer than a brother. He was Savior, Lord, Healer, and Deliverer. He was Redeemer and Refiner. He was Alpha and Omega, the Beginning and the End, the First and the Last. He was the Creator of the universe, the Creator of all things. His power was beyond description.

He was the Way, the Truth, and the Life. He was the Resurrection and the Life. He was the Messiah, the Anointed One. He was our great High Priest. He was our Mediator and Intercessor. He was the Great Shepherd, and the coming King. He was King of all Kings and Lord of all Lords.

He was the God of all Comfort. He was the Faithful and True Witness. He was the Amen. He was the God of Hope. He was our Wisdom and our Righteousness. He was the Father to the Fatherless. He was our beloved Bridegroom, and our Husband. He was the Light of the World. He was the Bread of Life.

He was our Rock, our Refuge, our Fortress, and our Shield. He was our Strong Tower. He was the King of Glory and the Ancient of Days. He was Emmanuel-God with us. His name was above all other names, and at the sound of his name, every knee bowed and every tongue confessed that He is Lord.

He was the Wonderful Counselor, Mighty God, Everlasting Father, and Prince of Peace. There was no end to the Increase of His Government. He was the One Who Was, Who Is, and Who is to Come. He was the Rose of Sharon, the Lily of the Valleys, and the Bright and Morning Star. He was Holy, and he was Just.

He was I Am! He was Love personified! He was Everything! He was all that we could ever want or need! He was the Beautiful One! He was the One we adore! He was the only one worthy of our praise!

I was completely undone. We who gathered there could do nothing except fall on our faces and worship him. We were so overcome by his beauty and majesty that we couldn't even speak. But our hearts were crying out to him with all the passion that was in us.

Then Jesus descended and came down into the church. He began walking down through the pews, and he transformed into whatever the person seated by him needed him to be. He appeared to one person as Jesus hanging on the cross. To another, he appeared as a friend. He appeared as a healer to others. He appeared as a father to some. He appeared as provision to others. To some, he appeared as a deliverer, breaking the chains of bondage around them.

He gave gifts to some, equipping them for the work of the ministry. To others he gave great comfort, strengthening them during their time of trial. He was a great encourager to some, and a counselor to others. And to all he offered his unconditional love.

He went through every pew in the church, appearing to each person in some manner that represented their need. He became everything to all people. He is everything! He is all we need. Jesus is everything to us. He is everything for us.

I wanted to share this with the church but was unable to speak at the time. I was completely overwhelmed! I did share this vision on a later date.

I pray that you would encounter Jesus for all he is.

Chapter 11
The Glory of the Cross

I was at an interdenominational men's retreat. It had started on a Thursday evening, and God was moving very powerfully in our midst. Being that men were there from many different denominations, we held a Mass on Saturday evening for the Catholics who were in attendance.

During the Mass, the priest asked if any of the Protestants wanted to come up and receive a blessing from him. Most, if not all of us, did. When the priest placed his hands on my head and blessed me, I felt a tremendous release of the power of God from him into me, and I began to travail. Travailing is much like the contractions that a woman experiences during childbirth.

I went back to my seat and told the Lord that I just wanted more of him. I wanted to know him better. I wanted more of his presence in my life. I wanted more of his power and glory to be manifested through me.

Then I began to think about the upcoming anointing service. Immediately after the Mass, we were going to hold an anointing service to pray for the sick, the oppressed, or for any other needs the men had. I said to the Lord that if he doesn't go with us, then don't send us out. There is no anointing apart from him.

I cried out to God from the depths of my heart and said that I wanted to see his glory. He replied, "This very night you shall see my glory." I started travailing much harder and was trembling all over. My entire body was shaking. I felt this tremendous heat come over me, and I began sweating profusely.

I felt that the Lord wanted me to be alone with him, so I asked some of the men to help me back to my bedroom. When they had gone, I asked the Lord what he was doing or what he was trying to show me. He asked me if I remembered the message that he had given me to speak to his people.

Instantly, I recalled the occasion back in 2002 and the message that God had given me to share. That encounter and message is found in chapter two of this book. After pondering that for a moment, the Lord said to me, "Now I will show you my glory."

I immediately found myself standing at the foot of the cross. I began to see flashbacks of all the beatings that Jesus took and all of the suffering that he went through for us. I saw him being punched, kicked, spit upon, and flogged.

I watched as they plucked the hair from his beard. It was almost more than I could bear to watch, but there was no way to stop it.

I tried closing my eyes, but the vision continued. I watched as they nailed Jesus to the cross. The pain that he endured was overwhelming to me. I saw the agony that he went through as he hung there. My heart was completely broken.

Despite all the suffering that he was going through, Jesus never stopped loving the people. When I looked into his eyes, I could still see the fire of his love for us. How could he love the people who were putting him through such agony? That's what unconditional love is. Jesus even went as far as to ask the Father to forgive them, because they didn't know what they were doing. Such amazing love!!

I also was able to see the Father looking down from heaven as all of this took place. At times, he looked as though he was in as much agony as Jesus was. I couldn't understand how he could bear it. But I also saw the same look of love in his eyes that I saw in the eyes of Jesus. Tears of pain were running down his face as he watched the beatings that Jesus took.

At the same time, tears of love for mankind and tears of joy because of the obedience of Jesus were also flowing from him. I, too, was in tears. There is no way you can watch the creator of the universe cry and not be moved to tears yourself. The Father was so proud of Jesus. Though it was very painful, he knew this had to be done in order for man to be saved.

Finally, when he had borne all of man's sin, infirmities, and sorrows, Jesus surrendered his life. It was finished. His body was taken down and moved to the tomb. The crowd dispersed, and the vision seemed to end. I was completely overwhelmed by the love of God.

After a few minutes of silence, I said to the Lord, "I thought you were going to show me your glory," a statement that I later regretted. He said, "I am." I didn't understand. He said, "The greatest display of my glory was when Jesus gave his life for all of mankind." I still didn't get it. Then he said, "My love is my glory. The greatest display of my glory was when I sent my son to the earth to redeem mankind and to restore the fellowship that was lost in the fall."

I finally got the revelation but felt like a complete idiot for asking such a dumb question after experiencing such a powerful thing. As I was pondering these things and contemplating just how much God loves us, he spoke to me again and said, "I love you as much as I love Jesus. I am love, and I love all people the same. It is impossible for me to love one person more than another, for I am love. It is who I am; it is what I am. I am love.

He continued, "By my very nature, it is impossible for me to love one more than another. At times, I may be more pleased with some than others, but my love for them remains the same. I can never love anyone any less or any more than I already do, for my love is perfect. You cannot improve upon perfection. Because of my great love for people, I was willing to sacrifice one so that a multitude could be saved. And I still ask some to make incredible sacrifices so that others can be saved."

He finished by charging me with this statement. "Go and tell my people how much I love them. Tell them that I was willing to sacrifice my son, a part of myself, so that I could have a personal relationship with each one of them. Implore them not to reject the offer I am making them. There are a few here this weekend who have not yet come into relationship with me."

Obviously, there are many people around the world who have not yet entered into relationship with the Father.

I was then returned to my bedroom, and after a few minutes to gather myself, I arose from my bed and wrote down the revelation.

I had always believed that God's glory was his fullness. It occurs whenever God's presence is manifested so powerfully that we begin to experience his love and his power in an overwhelming manner. For instance, in the Old Testament, the glory of the Lord filled the temple so powerfully that the priests could not even stand or minister. They were completely overwhelmed!

In Exodus 33, Moses asked God to show him his glory. The Lord replied that he would allow all his goodness to pass in front of him. God's glory is when his love, presence, power, and goodness are manifested on the earth to such a degree that mankind is overcome by it.

And there is no greater display of God's love, presence, power, and goodness than when Jesus died on the cross and was resurrected. Mankind has been completely overwhelmed by it for more than two thousand years!

I pray that you would experience the fullness of God's glory in your personal lives as only Jesus can reveal.

Chapter 12
Intercession

At times I wonder to myself if I am not crazy because of some of the things that I experience and some of the things that God asks me to do. But he assures me that I am not. He even leads me to scripture to confirm my madness! I felt the Lord leading me to share some of the things that I have done and experienced in the realm of intercession.

I could probably write an entire book about intercession, and maybe someday God will lead me to, but for now I will just share a few experiences. Let me start with Florida.

Tampa

My brother Chris and his wife, Patty, pastor a church near Tampa, Florida. A few years ago, early in 2008 if my memory is correct, they asked me to come down and minister at their church. A good friend of mine named Gary Nouse, who is an anointed worship leader, went with me.

We ministered on Friday and Saturday evenings as well as Sunday morning. But on Saturday morning we drove into downtown Tampa because Chris wanted us to see something. It was a huge painting titled *Leviathan*, hanging on a wall of a building. It was probably about forty feet high and twenty feet wide. It had hung there for many years.

This is what the writing on the painting said: "Before the earth was created, I am. I am lord over all the earth. No one can oppose me. I was there before man was created, and I always will be …"

The Lord immediately spoke to me and said that Leviathan was one of the chief principalities over Tampa. He told me that he wanted me to tear the principality down. I began seeking the Lord as to how to do it and also began interceding for Tampa. Later that day the Lord revealed to me that Leviathan was a water creature. He gave me a vision of stabbing my sword into a cup of water and making a proclamation against Leviathan.

So at the church service on Sunday morning, I did what the Lord had showed me to do. I pierced a cup of water with my sword and spoke the proclamation against Leviathan that the Lord had given to me. Sounds a little foolish, doesn't it? But God chooses the foolish things of the world to confound the wise.

Less than a week later, my brother Chris called me from Florida and told me that they had taken the *Leviathan* painting down. What a coincidence! Later that year, the

Tampa Bay Devil Rays baseball team changed their name to the Tampa Bay Rays. They took the devil out. Hmmmmm. Another coincidence? I think not.

I am foolish enough to believe God and do the things he shows me to do. And every time I do, incredible things happen.

New York

The Lord gave me a vision one time about another terrorist attack that was going to come through New York Harbor. He said that if we would go there and intercede, this attack could be stopped before it came to be. At times, God will reveal the schemes of the enemy to us so we can cut them off before they ever get started.

Through a very unique set of circumstances, God circumstances, we as a small group of people from very small towns in Pennsylvania found ourselves in the middle of New York City at the Brooklyn Tabernacle. I do not give glory to any man, but I do believe in honoring those whom God is using. Those who went with me were Dorey Marsh, Mary Emery, Darlene Murtland, Melissa Campbell, Cinda Sodmont, Teresa Wooley, and Kathy Thibodoux. We were certainly out of our comfort zone. The night we ended up at the Brooklyn Tabernacle was their regularly scheduled night of intercession. Imagine that.

During the service, the pastor called us forward as visitors from Pennsylvania and asked why we were there. We told him we came to intercede for the city and to squelch the plans of the enemy. He laid hands on all of us and blessed us and sent us out with full authority to do whatever it was that God led us to do. Wow, didn't see that one coming!

Later that night, they took us on a tour of the building. They took us up across a skywalk that overlooks the city. They told us that people who had been members there for many years had never seen the skywalk. What favor God bestowed on us!

Then when we were getting ready to leave, the head intercessor handed us a booklet about Daniel Nash, stating that God had told her to give it to us. I already mentioned Nash in chapter 8.

Incidentally, God later led us to go to the grave site of Daniel Nash to tap into his intercessory anointing. The day after we prayed at the grave site, gold dust appeared on Nash's name on his tombstone. I have a picture of it to this day.

The next morning, the Lord led us to go to Ground Zero to pray. It was very stark and sobering as we positioned ourselves away from the crowds so we could intercede in private. For the longest time, we stood there in silence. During that solemn time, I literally heard the voices of those who had perished there crying out to us and asking why we hadn't done more to warn them.

We then began to intercede out loud. We felt such love and mercy toward all those who had been affected. We also prayed that forgiveness would be extended to the perpetrators. By the time we had finished praying, a puddle of tears was on the concrete floor.

We then walked to New York Harbor to do what God would show us to do. It was a cold, breezy day, and we weren't properly dressed for the conditions. But we pressed on, stopping at times in different buildings to warm up a little. It seemed to take forever to get there, as we were walking directly into a pretty stiff wind.

We arrived at the harbor and stood gazing at the Statue of Liberty for a few moments. None of us knew how we were going to accomplish this task. The Lord had told me before we went that he was going to put his sword into the harbor to thwart the plans of the enemy. And as we stood there praying and asking God what to do, he said to me, "Rick, you are my sword. Thrust your arm into the water."

I then became a sword in the hand of the Lord. I thrust my arm into the water and made some prophetic declarations that the Lord was giving to me concerning the attack of the terrorists. I actually saw what looked like a torpedo leaving my hand and going out through the harbor to "blow up" the plans of the enemy.

Later that night, God had me enter the spiritual realm and deal with a principality that was actually behind these planned attacks. The Lord showed me that we are his gates, and what we allow on the earth will remain on the earth. But if we close the gates, or portals, to the enemy, then he cannot bring forth his plans on the earth. That night I closed the portal that this principality was coming through, and the enemy's scheme was defeated.

Hoover Dam

I am of the belief that sometimes, if not every time, when God shows us things that are about to come upon the earth, it is so we can intercede against them. For instance, in Exodus 32, God had shown Moses that he was going to destroy the Israelites because of their sin. However, Moses interceded, and God relented and did not bring upon Israel the disaster he had threatened.

I had heard of a vision by a well-known and accurate prophet of our day concerning some terrorist attacks coming upon America. One of those attacks concerned Hoover Dam. A few weeks later, while I was worshiping the Lord, I was caught up in the spiritual realm and was allowed to see some of the details of one of those attacks.

I saw a huge explosion at Hoover Dam, which caused the dam to break. I saw how everything that was downstream of the dam was destroyed. I saw the electricity going out in much of the western United States. I saw all kinds of looting, riots, and murder as a result of the loss of electricity. Many lives were destroyed. Then God spoke to me in the vision with these words:

Rick, this is not my judgment coming upon America. All judgment has been reserved until after the return of Christ. What you see before you is the work of the devil. And many of the natural disasters and destruction that you see all over the world are also the work of the devil. You are living under a new covenant, under grace, and are no longer under the law of sin and death.

But many people will continue to blame me for what is happening. Even many pastors and prophets will stand behind their pulpits and declare that this is my judgment coming upon the earth because of the wickedness of men. But they are wrong. They are hearing from the second heaven.

I take no delight in the death of the wicked, and I do not wish that any should perish. I came to give life, not destroy it. I did not come to judge the world, but to save it. These men will continue to give people the wrong image of who I am.

Because this is the work of the devil, it can be stopped, just like when Jesus would rebuke the storms, and they would cease. If my people will cry out to me in intercession, and use the authority that I have given them in the heavenly realms, these disasters do not have to happen. So tell my people to cry out on behalf of this nation, and I will thwart the plans of the enemy.

Later I felt the Lord leading me to go to Hoover Dam and intercede against this disaster. A number of very excellent people from my home church also felt led to go. Again I praise God for working through these people: Denise Disabato, Nadine Deitle, Mary Emery, Melia Lewis, Dorey Marsh, Darlene Murtland, and Pastor Kevin Stock.

We interceded over the next few weeks, with God showing us many things during that time. Then in February we flew to Las Vegas and from there traveled to Hoover Dam to intercede. We did everything God showed us to do, and we believe to this day that this disaster has been averted.

California

It has been prophesied over and over again both by believers and nonbelievers that one day California would suffer a huge earthquake along the San Andreas Fault and much of California would fall into the ocean. Even many scientists agree. Every time I heard this, something inside of me would rise up and say, "No, not on my shift."

Early in 2011, I felt the Lord leading me to travel to California and intercede against this natural/spiritual disaster. I began sharing these plans with others to see if anyone else felt led to go. Three others, Dave Deitle, Dorey Marsh, and Kathy Thibodoux, ended up traveling with me.

I was seeking the Lord to give me his strategy in the weeks leading up to the trip. My original thinking was to travel to somewhere in northern California to intercede, and then to visit the Bethel Church in Redding, where Bill Johnson and Kris Vallotton, two of my favorite teachers, are pastoring.

One day while praying over a map of California, I felt the Lord leading me to Palm Springs. I thought to myself, "Why Palm Springs?" Of all the places in California that we could have gone, Palm Springs would have been my last choice. I really felt we needed to go northwest of the city to pray, and also southeast of the city.

Dorey and Kathy both kept getting something about praying near or over the water. We thought at first that we were to go to the ocean, but that didn't fit with Palm Springs. We decided to go northwest and southeast of the city and see where God would lead us.

The enemy kept threatening me in the weeks leading up to the trip. Then, just a few days before the trip, two earthquakes, measuring 3.9 and 4.5 on the Richter Scale, hit California. One was centered northwest of Palm Springs, and the other was centered southwest of the city. Imagine that! Can you say, "Confirmation"?

We traveled to California, our flight being delayed in Denver because of a United Airlines computer glitch. However, we made it safely, contrary to the threats of the enemy, and did indeed travel northwest and southeast of the city to intercede.

We ended up at a remote location just off a major highway on the northwest side of the city. We prayed and made some declarations as the Lord led us. I planted my sword into the ground and prophesied against the coming destruction. When we felt released by the Lord from that location, we then headed southeast of the city.

As we were driving along, not sure where we were to even go, we saw a sign for the Salton Sea, and immediately I knew in my spirit that it was the proper place to intercede. An intercessor back home, Mary Emery, was praying over a map of California and called to tell us that we were supposed to go to the Salton Sea. Confirmation again.

It was the water that Dorey and Kathy had seen, and as it turns out, the fault line passes right under the sea. So we went there and once again planted my sword in the sea and made declarations contrary to the prophesies and beliefs of many people in this nation. We did everything we felt the Lord leading us to do on that trip, and we believe that our prayers combined with the prayers of others who believe these truths will avert this disaster.

I also received a major revelation from the Lord on that trip, some of which I will share in the next chapter of this book. These are just a few of many intercessory prayer assignments that the Lord has sent us on, and we have seen him do so many incredible things through our obedience.

O Lord, I pray that you would give the readers of this book a revelation of how intercession can change the outcome of things on earth so that they line up with the will of heaven.

Chapter 13
The Making of a Principality

It starts with one demon, one lie, and one person. The following vision and revelation is one that I received while on the intercessory prayer trip to California in 2011 that I mentioned in the previous chapter.

I was caught up in the Spirit where the Lord spoke to me and said, "Let me show you the making of a principality." Immediately I saw these events.

First, I saw the devil scheming with other demons to undermine the truth of God concerning creation. He was encouraging them to find a person of influence on the earth who would believe this lie of "evolution" and promote it until it had deceived many on the face of the earth.

This particular group of demons set out to accomplish this goal. One of them found their way to Charles Darwin. I watched in horror as the demon whispered the lie of evolution into Darwin's ear. At first, Darwin didn't believe it and didn't put much thought into it.

But the demon persisted in filling his head with this lie, even giving him thoughts, visions, and revelations about evolution. Darwin eventually succumbed to the lie. Not only did he start to believe it himself, he started sharing his new revelation with other people.

With each person that believed this new lie, the demon that started it seemed to get bigger and gain more strength and authority. As the demon grew, he gained influence over more and more people, and also over more and more other demons. Satan began to assign other demons to work with/ under this demon in promoting this new lie.

Today this one lie that started with one man and one demon is being taught in nearly every school in every nation of the world. Thousands have and are being deceived by this lie every day. And the demon that started it has grown into one of the most powerful and influential principalities on the earth.

If people believe the lie of evolution, that we evolved and are not created by a higher being, then there is no reason to worship or even communicate with that higher being. Instead, they end up worshiping the creation instead of the creator.

Since there is no God, and no one to answer to, then in a sense we all become gods unto ourselves. We can do whatever we want, to whomever we want, whenever we want, because we decide what's right for us. The result of people believing this lie is seen in the condition of the world today.

It has always been one of the schemes of the enemy to undermine God's truth with his lies. Scripture refers to him as the "father of all lies" in the book of John. Just as he lied to Adam and Eve in the garden to deceive them, he continues to lie to people today to deceive them and lead them away from the truth of God.

Jesus said that we would know the truth, and the truth would set us free. Satan doesn't want us to be free. So he fills our lives with lies in order to keep us in bondage.

The interesting thing that I noticed in this vision was that as people repeated the lie to others and more and more people believed the lie, the demon grew in power and influence.

> Proverbs 18:21: The tongue has the power of
> life and death.

We have the choice of either speaking the truth of God and promoting life, or speaking the lies of the enemy and promoting death. And most people don't realize how powerful our words are. They create realities in the spiritual realm that manifest into the physical realm.

For example, if I believe and speak that because heart disease runs in my family line I am also going to die from it, I am actually pronouncing a curse on myself and empowering the enemy to bring it to pass.

James chapter 3 says that with our tongues we praise God and also curse men. Every time we repeat the lies of the enemy with our tongues, we are cursing mankind. Not only that, we are giving life to the enemy and empowering him to bring forth his plans on the earth.

In believing the lie of the enemy, and repeating it to others, we are actually creating and strengthening principalities. We are empowering them to wreak havoc on the earth by coming into agreement with their lies. Ponder that for a moment.

Then the Lord showed me the principality that was in power over the fault line in California. He had spoken his lie to one influential person years ago, and now many on the face of the earth believe that California is going to suffer a huge earthquake and fall into the ocean.

Not only are scientists and geologists predicting this, but many in the church are saying the same. Prophets are actually prophesying these things. And every time they do, they empower the enemy to bring it to pass. I watched this particular principality grow exponentially because so many are believing his lie.

While I was in California, I saw the fear that many people are living under, just waiting for that day to come.

And every time we agree with the enemy, we feed the principality and cause him to grow.

It's bad enough that the unbelieving world has believed this lie, but it's even worse that many in the church are believing it. This may seem crazy, but the Lord showed me that the demon gains more strength from the church believing his lie than he does from the world.

As stated in the previous chapter, it is my belief that when God shows us these upcoming disasters, it's so we can intercede against them and prevent them from happening. We are not to come into agreement with them and empower the enemy to make it happen.

If this prophecy does come to pass some day, it will be because of the failure of the church to disagree with the enemy and intercede against it. Personally, I am of a mindset to say, "Not on my shift, Satan." I choose to come into agreement with Bethel Church and others in California and around the world and intercede against these disasters.

I pray that God would open your eyes to see the lies that you are living under so that you can be set free from them.

Chapter 14
Signs, Wonders, and Miracles

I guess no book about my encounters with God would be complete without including some of the testimonies of his great love, power, and glory that I have encountered over the years through signs, wonders, and miracles. I have had the privilege of seeing literally thousands of people saved, healed, and delivered by the power of God. Here are just a few.

Londrina, Brazil

I prayed for a woman in Londrina, Brazil, whose kidneys had completely failed her. She couldn't afford dialysis and was in desperate need of a transplant. She was very sickly looking and weak. She had to be assisted by two of her family members to even come forward for prayer. Her skin was yellow-looking.

I asked the Lord how to pray for her. I just had a sense to ask God to give her new kidneys, perhaps from the room that I had seen in chapter 1. All of a sudden, I looked up and saw two angels coming down with new kidneys in their hands. I watched in amazement as they removed her old kidneys and replaced them with new ones.

I didn't know what to say or do; I was so shocked at what I was seeing. Even after seeing all that I've seen, and receiving all the revelation that I have, I am still surprised at how God works. The only thing that came to my mind was to pray that her body would not reject these new kidneys and that there would be no infections.

I asked the woman if she was feeling anything. She said her kidneys were on fire. After a few minutes, her color began to change back to normal. Her strength came back to her body. She walked out of there under her own power looking like a completely different person than the one who had entered. Praise God!

The Lord then asked, "Why are you so surprised that I did what you asked of me?" I had no response. What could I possibly say?

Rome, New York

I was ministering at a church in New York. I had been prophesying to people while I was preaching, as I usually do. All of a sudden, I had a very strong urge to run to the back of the church and prophesy to a young man seated in the back pew. So I did.

As I quickly moved to the back of the church, I noticed three young boys sitting there. I wasn't sure which one it was, so I asked God. He said, "The one in the middle." So I began speaking a powerful word over him about his destiny. Tears were running down his face. When I finished, I returned to the front of the church and continued preaching.

Later that night, a woman who had been sitting next to him reported the following to me. Having heard the prophecy that I spoke over him, she commented to him, "That was a really good word, wasn't it?" The boy, age twelve, responded to her by telling this story.

"You have no idea what just happened here. I was walking up the road thinking about killing myself. When I saw the church service going on, I decided to come in. I sat here for awhile contemplating my life and thinking about ending it tonight. I watched that man speaking (prophesying) to other people, and I finally said to God, 'God, if you are real, and if you love me, then have that guy up there come back here and say something to me.' Before I was done speaking those words, he was already rushing back to me. When he spoke to me, I knew for the first time in my life that God was real and that he loved me."

During ministry time, the boy came forward and gave his heart to the Lord. Awesome! The following night he came back and was baptized in the Holy Spirit, speaking in tongues and having his body powerfully touched. What an awesome God we serve!

Ghana, Africa

I was ministering in Ghana, Africa. After preaching the gospel and leading a number of people to the Lord, we had prayer ministry time for anyone who needed healing or just wanted a touch from God. One of the women on the ministry team, Dulce Gerath, came over and asked me if I would come and pray with her for a fourteen-year–old boy who was born deaf. I said yes.

We went over and laid our hands on the boy's ears, and I prayed what I felt the Holy Spirit led me to pray. Then I asked him if there was any change. His father was with him, and they communicated through sign language. The boy said no.

We laid our hands on his ears and prayed again. This time, I literally felt the anointing flowing from me into him. When I asked him if there was any change, he again said no, but had a puzzled look on his face as if something was happening.

We laid our hands on his ears and prayed a third time. This time the boy said that while my hands were on his ears, he began to hear sound, but when I took them away, the sound went away.

I asked the Holy Spirit what was going on. He said it was a witchcraft curse put on the boy before he was born. I asked the Holy Spirit what I should do about it. He said, "Break it off of him."

So we placed our hands on his ears and prayed a fourth time, breaking the curse of witchcraft off of his life and body in the name of Jesus. When we had finished praying, I expected him to be able to hear. But his next comment, through sign language with his dad, was that he wanted to know Jesus as his Lord and Savior. I'll take that.

Then we prayed a fifth time, leading the boy through a prayer of salvation. Tears ran down his cheeks as he met Jesus for the first time. This boy had just been saved and delivered from the curse of witchcraft. Pretty good night! But I sensed God wasn't finished with him yet.

We placed our hands on his ears and prayed again. Number six. I said, "I command these ears to open in the name of Jesus." When I took my hands away, the boy's face lit up like a Christmas tree. He smiled from ear to ear. For the first time in his life, he could hear! And the first word he ever heard was, of course, Jesus! There's just something about that name!

If we had quit praying after the third time, the boy would still be lost, deaf, and under the curse of witchcraft. But because we persisted, he is now saved, healed, and delivered! Thank you, Jesus!

We later received a report that one of the pastors was teaching the boy how to speak.

Ebensburg, Pennsylvania

Now I want to share the testimony of Jim, Jill, and Cody Castiglione, a family whose lives have been powerfully touched by the love and grace of God. This is the testimony that they shared with me one evening.

Jill had an accident where she fell about eight to ten feet off a deck and landed on the back of her head on a concrete pad. Their lives would dramatically change for nearly ten years as a result of this accident.

Jill suffered extreme pain from migraines nearly every day for the next nine and a half years. From three to five days a week, she would be so "out of it" that she barely was able to get out of bed, except to use the bathroom. She would fall over at times, would fall into deep "pseudo stares" (her terminology) in which she would enter a trancelike stare that nobody could bring her out of at times, and would talk delirious at other times.

She suffered many seizures and convulsions that were brought on by the pain of the migraines. Because of all of this, she could not be left alone. She had to have someone watching her at all times. Jim, her husband, and Cody, her son, carried the brunt of this burden. Cody was only three and a half years old when this happened, and he ended up taking care of his mother more than she was able to care for him. Cody told me that though he felt bad for his mom, he really wasn't upset with her or disappointed in her in any way.

They had prayed and been prayed for numerous times, but each time the healing didn't come they became more and more discouraged. Jill came to the point where she thought she would be better off dead than to live like this. She was deeply saddened that she missed so much of Cody's life. She wondered where God was in all of this.

Jim and Cody had pretty much resigned themselves to the fact that this was what the rest of their lives was going to be like. Jim had actually felt that it would be better for his wife to pass on than to live like this the rest of her life.

Enter God! I was holding a healing service at the Crossroads Alliance Church in Ebensburg, Pennsylvania. A good friend of mine, Dave Deitle, who was also friends with Jim and Jill, had invited them to come to the service to receive prayer.

The day of the service, Jill was very sick. She had severe headaches, seizures, and vomiting. She told Jim that there was no way she could go in that condition. The service started at 7:00 p.m., and finally, at about 6:45 p.m., Jill decided she would try to go.

They arrived at the church at about 7:30 p.m., and we were already deeply involved in worship. I was lying on the floor in the front of the church receiving revelation from the Lord. Others were dancing, waving flags, and just worshiping the way we were accustomed to.

But for Jim, Jill, and Cody, this was all new and much different than anything they had ever experienced. Cody asked Jill why that guy was lying on the floor and stated that he wanted to leave. Jim was very uncomfortable and worried for Jill. Loud noise typically triggered her migraines, and the worship that night was certainly loud and extravagant. Jim actually took earplugs and had Jill wear them during worship, hoping she wouldn't be triggered.

They were all shocked when I arose from the floor and introduced myself as the speaker. They wondered what their friend Dave had gotten them into.

But as I was lying on the floor, the Lord had given me three words of knowledge for healing for three different people. Jill was one of them. I had actually seen her face in a vision, and when I looked over the crowd and saw Jill sitting there, I was excited. I knew God wanted to heal her that night.

I immediately began to minister to the three people for whom God had given me word. When I prayed for Jill, I spoke everything according to what God had shown me, declaring that God was reconnecting the circuits in her brain that had been damaged in the accident and other things like that. I felt such a love in my heart for her. It was God's love. And there was so much heat on my hands as I placed them on Jill; I felt sure she would be healed.

But she wasn't. Jim and Cody asked her if anything had happened. When she said no, they were discouraged again. It was just another in a long line of failed prayers. They were all a little freaked out by the manifestation of the Spirit upon me, having never seen anything like that. They thought about leaving, but praise God they didn't.

In my heart, I knew that God wanted to heal her. As I continued ministering to others that night and preaching the gospel, I kept asking God in my spirit to do whatever it took to break through for Jill's healing. About a half hour later, God downloaded a prophetic word to me for Jill.

I went back to her, placed my hands on her head and began prophesying to her. God laid bare the secrets of her heart, calling out a list of symptoms and feelings that Jill knew I could not have known, except by the Spirit of God. Jim could actually feel the anointing on me.

When I was finished, Jim and Cody once again asked her how she felt. Jill exclaimed, "It's gone; it's gone." The pain that she had lived with for nearly ten years was suddenly gone. Cody began to cry tears of joy. Jim was wondering if this could really be real, after all these years. Could Jill really be healed?

Jim and Jill were afraid to go to sleep that night, fearing that when Jill woke up, the pain would be back. But it wasn't! Hallelujah! Praise God! Cody kept asking Jill all week if she had any headaches, but to this day Jill remains healed.

Since that time, I have become good friends with Jim and Jill. They are attending a ministry class that I teach, and they travel on ministry trips with me, sharing their testimony and praying for others to be healed. Jill's face shines like the noonday sun as she shares her testimony and ministers to others. Cody, who is now sixteen, even shares his testimony with his friends.

Jim has said that he got his wife back and his life back. Cody said it's really cool having his mom back. God is good, all the time. All glory belongs to him alone!

I pray that the healing power of the Holy Spirit would flow through you right now to bring healing to every area of your body and life in the name of Jesus!

Chapter 15
Encountering Christ

Through the course of this book, I have shared some incredible testimonies with all of you. I have also shared some of the revelation that I have received through these encounters. But I also intentionally did not share some revelations with you, hoping that the testimony itself would cause a hunger in you to seek out revelation yourself.

John 19:10 declares that the testimony of Jesus is the spirit of prophecy. Every testimony that is given is an invitation from God to the reader/hearer to encounter him in the same manner. If you hear a testimony of healing, it is an invite for you to be healed. As I have shared some of my testimonies, you are being invited to encounter God in similar ways.

I believe part of God's desire in having me write this book, is to give others an opportunity to get to know him better by encountering him like I have. After all, knowledge without an encounter becomes nothing more than mere religion.

Let me ask you a couple of questions. Why do you go to church? Why do you pray? Why do you read/study the Bible? Why do you do any of the religious activities that you do? Do you simply do these things because that's what Christians do? Are you just trying to fulfill your Christian duties? Or do you do them intentionally, with a sincere desire to know and encounter the living Christ?

You see, you could memorize the entire Bible and still not know God. All you would have is a lot of facts about God in your head. But when you actually encounter him, that knowledge becomes revelation that changes your life. It becomes truth that sets you free. Consider the words of Jesus to the Jews.

> John 5:39–40
>
> You diligently study the Scriptures because you think that by them you possess eternal life. These are the Scriptures that testify about me,
>
> Yet you refuse to come to me to have life.

The Pharisees of Jesus's day had spent their entire lives studying and memorizing the scriptures. But when the Son of God was actually standing right in front of them, they did not recognize him. All of their religion had blinded them to the truth of who was right in front of them.

I don't want you to walk away from this book thinking that I am more important or more spiritual than you. I want to encourage you to believe that you can experience God in supernatural ways yourself. This book is an invitation for you to encounter the living Christ. It's an opportunity for you to get to know him better.

I pray, like Paul, that God would give you a spirit of wisdom and revelation that you might know him better. There is no greater thing! If all of our religious activity does not lead us to encounter and know him better, we are completely missing the point.

What God desires the most is to simply have a relationship with us. He desires to fellowship with us. He desires us to be intimate with him. And then, out of intimacy and relationship, he will show us what he wants us to do with our lives. It's much more than just fulfilling our religious duties, or keeping the traditions of our church, or believing man-made doctrines.

God has a specific plan and purpose for all of us. He has put each of us on this planet to fulfill a specific destiny. And only when we encounter him, know him, and live in intimacy with him, can we begin to discover and fulfill our destinies.

Consider how the Apostle Paul viewed these things. He had spent a large part of his life as a Pharisee, yet for all of his religion, he did not know Christ. He was actually persecuting and putting to death the followers of Jesus, until he himself encountered Christ on the road to Damascus.

He later stated that he now considered all of his religion nothing but garbage compared to knowing Jesus. That's a pretty strong statement!

Philippians 3:4–11:

If anyone else thinks he has reasons to put confidence in the flesh, I have more:

Circumcised on the eighth day, of the people of Israel, of the tribe of Benjamin, a Hebrew of Hebrews; in regard to the law, a Pharisee;

As for zeal, persecuting the church; as for legalistic righteousness, faultless.

But whatever was to my profit I now consider loss for the sake of Christ.

What is more, I consider everything a loss compared to the surpassing greatness of knowing Christ Jesus my Lord, for whose sake I have lost all things. I consider them rubbish, that I may gain Christ

And be found in him, not having a righteousness of my own that comes from the law, but that which is through faith in Christ—the righteousness that comes from God and is by faith.

I want to know Christ and the power of his resurrection and the fellowship of sharing in his sufferings, becoming like him in his death,

And so, somehow, to attain to the resurrection from the dead.

What about you? Do you have a relationship with Jesus? Are you getting to know him more and more? Do you live intentionally, for the purpose of knowing him and fulfilling his destiny for your life? Do you encounter him on a regular basis, or are you just going through the motions of religion?

God does not want your religion; he wants you! He wants to be your friend. He wants to be your Father. He wants to be your beloved. He wants you to encounter him, to know him intimately. He wants you to be saved, healed, and delivered. He wants you to be free. He sent his Son to die for you so that you could have these things.

Don't settle for anything less. Give yourself fully to the Lord. Don't let anything that Jesus purchased for you go to waste. Fulfill your destiny!

I pray for all of you, that you would have the same type of kingdom encounters that I have had. I pray that you would truly encounter the living Christ!

Contact Information

Richard A. Sodmont

834 Number Nine Road

Hastings, PA 16646

(814) 247-8645

or

(814) 243-7580

E-mail: hhlm@live.com